D0934640

Economics as a
Coordination Problem

Economics as a Coordination Problem

The Contributions of Friedrich A. Hayek

Gerald P. O'Driscoll, Jr.

Foreword by
F. A. Hayek

SHEED ANDREWS AND MCMEEL, INC.
Subsidiary of Universal Press Syndicate
Kansas City

This edition is cosponsored by the Institute for
Humane Studies, Inc., Menlo Park, California, and
Cato Institute, San Francisco, California.

Economics as a Coordination Problem
Copyright© 1977 by the Institute for Humane Studies.

Library of Congress Cataloging in Publication Data

O'Driscoll, Gerald P
  Economics as a coordination problem.

  (Studies in economic theory)
  A revision of the author's thesis, University of
California at Los Angeles.
  Bibliography: p.
  Includes index.
  1. Hayek, Friedrich August von, 1899-   2. Austri-
an school of economists.   3. Economics—History.
I. Title. II. Series.
HB101.H39037 1977   330'.092'4   77-23382
ISBN 0-8362-0662-2
ISBN 0-8362-0663-0 pbk.

To Lyla,

with affection

CONTENTS

FOREWORD

On the Way

To give a coherent account of the whole of the theoretical work of an economist who has not attempted to do so himself is sometimes a useful task. But the proof of its worthwhileness must be that the attempt at systematization leads beyond the point where the author discussed left off. On this standard Professor O'Driscoll, if the task he has undertaken was worth doing at all, has done it very well indeed.

It is a curious fact that a student of complex phenomena may long himself remain unaware of how his views of different problems hang together and perhaps never fully succeed in clearly stating the guiding ideas which led him in the treatment of particulars. I must confess that I was occasionally myself surprised when I found in Professor O'Driscoll's account side by side statements I made at the interval of many years and on quite different problems, which still implied the same general approach. That it seems in principle possible to recast a great part of economic theory in terms of the approach which I had found useful in dealing with such different problems as those of industrial fluctuations and the running of a socialist economy was the more gratifying to me as what I had done had often seemed to me more to point out barriers to further advance on the path chosen by others than to supply new ideas which opened the path to further development. Professor O'Driscoll has almost persuaded me that I ought to have continued with the work I had been doing in the 1930s and 1940s rather than let myself be drawn away to other problems which I felt to be more important. I cannot now really regret it, however, when I see that not only he but also a few others are pushing beyond the point where my own impetus had flagged; in fact their efforts are doing more to make me think again about those problems than I would otherwise have done.

F. A. Hayek
Obergurgl, Austria
September, 1975

PREFACE

In writing this book, I decided in general not to consult with Professor Hayek. If the reinterpretation was to be authentic and worthwhile, it would necessarily involve my piecing together his ideas as they were presented and available. I wanted to assess Hayek's contributions, not what Hayek himself *recalled* contributing, or *intended* to contribute. I was thus especially pleased that when he gave me his impressions of the penultimate draft in the form of a foreword, he found my interpretation satisfactory.

There are many people who deserve thanks for the assistance that they have rendered. If it is possible to make such a judgment, my greatest intellectual debt is to Axel Leijonhufvud. This debt is far greater than the usual one to the chairman of one's dissertation committee. During the period of time I was at U.C.L.A., he was always available to give advice on a wide range of problems. He seemed to have an infinite supply of time, and a way of avoiding the inessentials and moving right to the heart of a problem. Much of what is worthwhile in this book is due to what I learned in and out of the classroom from him, and to his stern criticisms of earlier drafts of my Ph.D. dissertation. He is to be especially absolved from responsibility for any remaining errors, as I am quite aware of the areas where we disagree.

Professor Robert Clower was also willing to give of his time whenever asked for assistance. Since Professor Clower does not have the dubious distinction of ever having been officially associated with this project, he is certainly protected from all blame. But my appreciation for his assistance, rendered at critical junctures, cannot be adequately expressed. I would also like to thank the other members of my dissertation committee, Professors Sam Peltzman and Thomas Sowell, for the help they rendered along the way.

My experience at U.C.L.A. provided great intellectual stimulation. The constellation of great minds was truly awe inspiring. One had the sense of economics being once again made a lively and interesting field in which to work. This sense of excitement was infectious, and the graduate students greatly benefited. It would be impossible to name all of the faculty and staff who, in discussions and otherwise, provided help and stimulation.

The economics department at Iowa State University proved to be a very congenial place in which to carry forth the preparation of this book from my dissertation. Dudley Luckett has helped in ways he undoubtedly does not realize, by his willingness to discuss subjects whose connection with this book he could not then have known. I early learned that the *cognoscenti* in the department attended Charles Meyer's informal luncheon seminars in the Cardinal Room. I have benefited immensely from the many discussions he and I have had over lunch and at other times.

Professor Israel Kirzner gave encouragement and aid for this project at a time when they were both needed. Professor Ludwig M. Lachmann was also kind enough to read and comment on my dissertation. I very much appreciate the help that both of them have rendered.

The Liberty Fund provided me with a fellowship for the summer of 1975, for which I am profoundly grateful. This fellowship not only enabled me to attend to my typescript full time, but put me in the company of other scholars interested in the same general area. As part of the fellowship, I spent the summer at the Institute for Humane Studies in Menlo Park, California. I benefited from the helpful comments of the other fellows, including Roger Garrison, Richard Ebeling, and Gary and Eugenie Short. Miss Sudha R. Shenoy, in particular, deserves thanks for having read and edited the dissertation in its entirety. George Pearson and Kenneth S. Templeton, Jr., of the Institute for Humane Studies arranged for this program. Neil McLeod of the Liberty Fund saw to the funding. And the staff of the Institute, particularly Ellen Burton and Martha Heitkamp, saw to it that all went smoothly. I wish to thank all of them.

The Liberty Fund's summer program enabled me to meet Professor Hayek for the first time, as he was a Senior Fellow in the program. It was particularly stimulating to meet him at that time, as he was in the midst of writing his three volume magnum opus, *Law, Legislation and Liberty*.

Professor Murray N. Rothbard is largely responsible for interesting me in the contributions of the Austrian school. One might say that he predisposed me to write this work. He himself has contributed to the tradition, and his works were often valuable sources for further references. He also read and commented on my dissertation, for which I am especially grateful.

As the deadline for delivery of the typescript approached, the third floor typing staff in the economics department at Iowa State University performed heroic feats, beyond the call of duty. Mrs. Betty Ingham organized a veritable typing brigade. Denise Collins, Diana Grimm, Mrs. John Kooistra, and she typed furiously and efficiently, even at night and on weekends. There is no way that I can express my appreciation for what they did. And I am most grateful to the department for providing such fine support.

My wife, Lyla, was more than the proverbial constant source of support. She took an active part in editing and rewriting at various stages. And she did this despite the fact that she at all times had her own work to do. I gratefully dedicate this book to her.

Gerald P. O'Driscoll, Jr.
Santa Barbara, California
February 1976

INTRODUCTION

Axel Leijonhufvud first suggested to me that reexamining Hayek's contributions might be worthwhile. From the start, I sensed that Hayek's theories were misunderstood in important respects. One major reason was the tidal wave of the Keynesian revolution. Contributing to the eager acceptance of Keynes's message was a desperate desire for a cure for the economic ills of the Great Depression.

The orthodox economics of the 1930s seemed incapable of guiding policymakers, although even the textbooks of the day did deal with the problem of unemployment which was of so much concern to policymakers (see J. Ronnie Davis, *The New Economics and the Old Economists* [Ames, Ia.: Iowa State University Press, 1971]). Then, however, as now in crisis situations economists were more likely to abandon economic principles entirely than to reformulate them.

Without becoming embroiled in the Keynes and the Keynesians debate (see Axel Leijonhufvud, *On Keynesian Economics and the Economics of Keynes* [New York: Oxford University Press, 1968]), I believe it is important to point out how most economists—particularly most American economists—received Keynes's message. With the adoption of Keynesian economics, the difficult problems of monetary and capital theory that occupied the profession during the entire post-World War I period would be simplified. By supposing that aggregate consumption is a function of current (national) income and that savings and investment together determine the level of national income, the world suddenly was made intelligible in very simple terms. Such issues as "forced saving," the difference between the money and natural rates of interest, and the investment period became irrelevant.

I cannot overemphasize that the Keynesian revolution also had profound and unfortunate effects on economic research. The profession lost interest in a whole range of issues to which the major theorists of the day had made important contributions (see Fritz Machlup, "Friedrich von Hayek's Contribution to Economics," *Swedish Journal of Economics* 76 [1974]: 508-509). Consequently, in the nine years between the publication of Keynes's *General Theory* and the end of World War II, the fortunes of various economists changed remarkably. These changes occurred much more rapidly, for instance, than did the acceptance of the so-called marginal revolution at the end of the nineteenth century (see Mark Blaug, "Kuhn versus Lakatos, or Paradigms Versus Research Programmes in the History of Economics," *History of Political Economy* 7 [Winter 1975]: 399-433).

In the Keynesian revolution Hayek was not merely misunderstood—he was victimized by myth making. With the acceptance of Keynesian economics, the history of economics was rewritten. Economics was divided into pre–Keynesian and Keynesian thought (and now we speak of post–Keynesian economics). Accepting Keynes's own solecistic usage, economists perceived Keynes's predecessors—with a few exceptions—as "classical" economists. In keeping with Keynes's original suggestion, Oskar Lange pictured economists before Keynes as believing in Say's law of markets (Oskar Lange, "Say's Law: A Restatement and Criticism," in Oskar Lange et al. eds., *Studies in Mathematical Economics and Econometrics* [Chicago: University of Chicago Press, 1942]). Belief in Say's law became, then, the hallmark of the classical system and the alleged source of all the great classical errors. Say's law not only was reinterpreted in a way that made it scarcely recognizable to an authentic classical economist, but also was made into a proposition that only a fool would accept. This defamation of Keynes's predecessors is what, I believe, Keynes and, even more, his followers accomplished in a decade (see W. H. Hutt, *A Rehabilitation of Say's Law* [Athens, Ohio: Ohio University Press, 1974]).

Classificatory *schema* of the "Keynesian–classical" variety are suspect to say the least. The lumping together of virtually all

Keynes's predecessors obscures what distinguishes economists between the Marginal Revolution and the Keynesian revolution. Overlooked in particular are the many and diverse contributions to the theory of economic fluctuations by monetary specialists from the end of the nineteenth century to the 1930s and beyond. These economists include, *inter alia*, Ludwig von Mises, Gunnar Myrdal, D. H. Robertson, Hayek, and even Keynes himself in his *Treatise on Money* (1st ed., 1930 in *The Collected Writings of John Maynard Keynes*, vols. 5 and 6 [London: Macmillan & Co., 1971]). Each of these economists pointed to the failings of the quantity theory and offered revisions. They also contributed to the development of the theory of economic fluctuations. It is therefore misleading to describe them as classical or pre–Keynesian. Also these theorists developed certain parts of what is termed Keynes's critique of monetary economics to a greater extent than Keynes himself did.

There are, then, two basic reasons for reexamining Hayek's work today. First, a reassessment of his position in the development of economics is long overdue. His positive contributions to contemporary economic theory have not been fully appreciated. His ideas, which were pushed into the shadows of the Keynesian revolution, are no longer summarized in the leading textbooks. Second, the failure of current Keynesian or post–Keynesian theories of economic fluctuations to explain satisfactorily the simultaneous occurrence of inflation and unemployment makes what Hayek said about this phenomenon seem more important.

My claim that Hayek was misunderstood by his contemporaries requires amplification. The Austrian school (of which Hayek was the leading representative at that time in Britain) had a foreign flavor to which British economists were unaccustomed. Furthermore, the lack of understanding led to a failure among Anglo–American economists to comprehend the larger import of Hayek's message. Hayek called for an entire restructuring of economic theory. In part, he was attempting to counter the revived interest in the general equilibrium theories—the neo–Walrasian and neo–Paretian theories of the 1930s as found, for example, in John R. Hicks's writings. However, economics, even before the widespread adoption of general equilibrium models, had unfortunately become virtually a branch of mechanics. The important problem of finding the social institutions that best coordinate economic activities had been lost sight of. Adam Smith, in his notion of the "invisible hand," called attention to the complex manner in which a prosperous social order is produced, although no one individual (or group of individuals) designed that order or intended that it be produced. Building on Smith, Carl Menger, the founder of the Austrian school, defined economics (and social science in general) as the study of the *unintended* consequences of human action. Hayek here followed in Smith's and Menger's footsteps.

In Hayek's view, economics begins where direct observation leaves off. The immediate impact of most economic decisions is apparent even to the untrained: a legal control holding price below the market-clearing price makes goods less expensive (in money terms); a minimum wage set above the market–clearing level raises the income of (employed) workers. Economics deals with the hidden aspects of these problems, or phenomena not readily understood to be aspects of these problems (for example, shortages and unemployment).

In this view, economics is intimately concerned with institutions—social, political, and economic; for it is these institutions that shape the operative economic forces and determine the outcome. Economics must then be theoretical *and* institutional if it is to elucidate social phenomena. Whether a satisfactory economic order will emerge depends on the operation of these institutions and thus on their precise nature. Individual decision making and market prices may or may not produce coordinated results; the outcome depends on the functioning of these institutions. Economic systems, market or otherwise, simply do not work in isolation. These insights have gained wider acceptance in recent years. But the realization that institutions matter all too often involves grafting *ad hoc* observations on to a theory in which institutions are not strictly relevant.

Economic institutions exist largely to facilitate the dissemination of information among actors. The study of the development of economic order depends, then, on assumptions concerning the flow of information. Standard theorems of resource allocation are only the starting point. Hayek often criticized economists for generally ignoring this institutional–informational problem.

In his lectures at the University of London in 1931 (Friedrich A. Hayek, *Prices and Production,* 2d ed. [London: Routledge & Kegan Paul, 1935]), Hayek appeared to be discussing recondite matters in monetary and capital theory. His subject matter, however, was unusually topical in light of the Great Depression. While his conclusions were provocative, these lectures were apparently unrelated to the wider problems of economic planning or to his other work on economic information. Yet they were intimately related, although writers continue to compartmentalize his work rather than study it in its entirety.

Hayek himself never demonstrated how all his ideas "hang together." Although this study is restricted to his economic writing, Hayek's later work on political and legal philosophy and even on the philosophy of perception is consistent with his earlier work on technical economics. A comprehensive treatment of Hayek's contributions might demonstrate that his book on economic fluctuations in 1931 led him to write *Law, Legislation, and Liberty* in the 1970s!

Secondary source material proved a poor guide for understanding Hayek's ideas. While I do not ignore the secondary source material, I restrict myself to what I consider to be the important errors of interpretation. I have also avoided any direct discussion of the Hayek–Frank H. Knight debates on the meaning and definition of capital. These debates are ancillary to the main theme of this book, though by no means irrelevant. Furthermore, Knight did not offer a theory of capital at all, in the sense of a theory of adjustment and investment in disequilibrium (see M. Northrup Buechner, "Frank Knight on Capital as the Only Factor of Production," *Journal of Economic Issues* 10 [September 1976]: 598-617). Rather, Knight's central argument about capital—that no sense can be made of a period of production or investment because of the simultaneity of production and consumption—really involved a series of tautologous propositions about the stationary state. Many have made this point, but none more forcefully than Fritz Machlup, who, moreover, pointed out that when Knight conceded—as he did—that disinvestment is possible, he conceded the whole argument to the Austrians (see Fritz Machlup, "Professor Knight and the 'Period of Production'," *Journal of Political Economy* 43 [October 1935]: 579-80).

In order that my remark that Knight's theory is not a theory of capital be understood, I shall quote from Hayek's own characterization of his endeavor in *The Pure Theory of Capital*:

Our main concern will be to discuss in general terms what type of equipment it will be most profitable to create under various conditions, and how the equipment existing at any moment will be used, rather than to explain the factors which determined the value of a given stock of productive equipment and of the income that will be derived from it. [P. 3]

Whatever Knight's "theory of capital" was, it was not a theory of capital in this sense. To offer it as an alternative to Hayek's theory is akin to offering a theory of supply as an alternative to a theory of demand. As Ludwig M. Lachmann has reminded us, we still do not have a theory of capital, though interest theories, misnamed "theories of capital," do go under this title (see L. M. Lachmann, "Reflections on Hayekian Capital Theory" [New York: mimeographed, 1975]).

To reiterate, the main theme of this book is the coordination of economic activities. Hayek's work is seen as variations of this theme. And taken together, his work is viewed as providing a basis for a radical alternative to the "neoclassical" paradigm of efficient allocation with timeless production, perfect anticipations, costless exchanges, (almost) instantaneous attainment of equilibrium, and a world of no institutions. In many ways, Hayek and his fellow Austrians harked back to classical political economy. But being subjective-value theorists and methodological individualists, they rejected the objective-value theory and methodological holism of Ricardian political economy. In doing so, they advanced the basic research program of Adam Smith. They shared with the Institutionalists a concern for the evolution of market institutions, but viewed this study as complementary to, rather than a substitute for, economic theory. They were foremost among the theorists of their day, but resisted limiting economics to the pure theory of equilibrium states. In the pages that follow, I hope to support these characterizations by explicating both the specific contributions and general approach of Hayek in particular. In doing so I will emphasize his monetary economics, wherein lie his greatest technical contributions. But since to do so would virtually falsify my own thesis, I will by no means limit myself to monetary economics. Instead, I will attempt to connect his many and diverse contributions to economics, and to show that they evidence an overall conception of economics as the study of decentralized planning and market coordination.

1

The Controversies of the 1920s

Cultivation of the history of thought is more necessary in economics than in the natural sciences because earlier discoveries in economics are more in danger of being forgotten; maintaining a *cumulative* growth of knowledge is more difficult. In the natural sciences, discoveries get embodied not only in further advances in pure knowledge but also into technology, many of whose users have a profit–and–loss incentive to get things straight. The practitioners of economic technology are largely politicians with rather different motives. (Analogies between the market test and the ballot–box test have been fashionable in recent years, but the differences should not be forgotten.) In economics, consequently, we need scholars who specialize in keeping us aware of earlier contributions and so enable us to recognize earlier successes— and earlier mistakes—when they surface as supposedly new ideas. By exerting a needed discipline, specialists in the history of thought can contribute to the cumulative character of economics (Leland B. Yeager, "The Keynesian Diversion," *Western Economic Journal* 11 [June 1973:1]63).

INTRODUCTION

The name John Maynard Keynes and the brand of economics that is called "Keynesian" are known to every practicing economist and economics student today. In contrast the work of Friedrich A. Hayek is practically unknown to the present generation. To older economists the name "Hayek" is but a reminder of past debates. Until the 1974 award of the Nobel Memorial Prize in economics (jointly to Professors Hayek and Myrdal) economists had lost interest in his works. Sir John Hicks commented on the neglect of Hayek's work:

When the definitive history of economic analysis during the nineteen–thirties comes to be written, a leading character in the drama (and it was quite a drama) will be Professor Hayek. Hayek's economic writings . . . are almost unknown to the modern student; it is hardly

1

remembered that there was a time when the new theories of Hayek
were the principal rival of the new theories of Keynes. Which was right,
Keynes or Hayek? There are still living teachers of economics, and
practical economists, who have passed through a time when they had to
make up their minds on the question; and there are many of them
(including the present writer) who took quite a time to make up their
minds.[1]

Hicks asked, "How was it that this happened?" I feel that there
is ample reason to take up Hicks's query, quite apart from an
interest in the development of contemporary economic theory
or in the reasons for present-day neglect of research problems
once considered important. Such an inquiry may reveal new
knowledge or, more precisely, as Yeager pointed out, may redis-
cover what the profession as a whole has forgotten.

Scientific development is typically viewed as a cumulative
process of hypothesis formation, empirical testing, hypothesis
reformulation, retesting, and so on. This process systematically
rejects unsubstantiated hypotheses and accepts hypotheses not
found inconsistent with the evidence. Over time, textbooks in
each field incorporate important discoveries and delete past
errors. At any given time a particular science embodies all ideas
and theories currently known to be true and excludes those
known to be untrue.

It has been argued that this description of scientific discovery
is inaccurate. In a pathfinding work, T. S. Kuhn suggested that a
science develops by a way of "revolutions."[2] Day–to–day scientific activity is seen as "filling the empty boxes" of accepted
theory with empirical content. An accepted body of theory together with an accepted research methodology constitutes what
Kuhn called a "scientific paradigm."

Kuhn's view recognizes the impossibility of treating all pre-
conceptions and theorems as propositions subject to rejection at
any time. In any science, then, there is a "core," a body of theory
not subject to dispute and a body of factual information accepted
as true. One need only speculate on the state of economic knowledge if supply–and–demand analyses were treated as hypotheses, ever subject to testing and rejection. On the other hand, the
prevailing orthodoxy influences scientists' perceptions and

judgments; some questions are not raised or, if raised, are not to be regarded as "scientifically proper." As a consequence, certain avenues of investigation are unexplored, and theoretical errors go undiscovered.

In Kuhn's analysis, the scientific paradigm is abandoned when anomalous research results make it increasingly difficult to maintain the paradigm intact. Such findings may at first be rejected because they do not fit into orthodox theory, though other reasons may be given. Indeed, the discoverers may find themselves beyond the pale of science precisely because their findings are anomalous. Eventually, however, the paradigm cannot be maintained in the face of ever–increasing evidence. A new paradigm must be constructed, and since the resources of the profession are devoted to debating paradigms, scientific progress is retarded until a new orthodoxy emerges.

If this Kuhnian view is correct, there are two disturbing consequences. First, in the rejection of an established paradigm some knowledge may be lost; all verities in the old paradigm need not necessarily be incorporated into a new paradigm. Second, a paradigm may be rejected on the basis of anomalous findings although these findings can be made consistent with that paradigm. These insights will be made use of in this book.

Work by economists reexamining the so-called Keynes–versus–the–classics debate has led to another debate, one that might be termed the Keynes–and–the–Keynesians debate.[3] Economists refer to both Keynes's *General Theory* and the ensuing debates as the Keynesian Revolution. The word *revolution* implies a radical break with previous tradition. Early work on this revolution dealt with what Keynes was really saying and with how much and where it differed in general terms from what his predecessors had said. Interest then shifted to what Keynes's predecessors really said: was there truly a "classical economics" or was this simply a straw man to make Keynes's writings look significant.[4]

An early finding of the original Keynes–versus–the–classics debate was that classical economics had never produced a consistent theory on macro issues. Hicks pointed this out as early as 1937, though writers of macro textbooks have since shown great ingenuity in constructing a "classical economics" out of whole cloth. As a result of these investigations, it can be argued that Keynes not only made no major theoretical contributions but also made no original policy prescriptions. Indeed, Axel Leijonhufvud suggested that Keynes broke with the established paradigm of economics insofar as he focused on "income–constrained" processes, but that his theoretical contributions were perhaps not as innovative as his more exuberant followers would have it.[5] For one, Keynes remained at heart a Marshallian; Marshallian economics was the only economics he really knew well. Leijonhufvud also argued that the innovative aspect of Keynes's work lay elsewhere than in the areas covered in a standard Keynesian work. Keynes was innovative in his broad conception of how a market system operates and how it may break down.[6]

Keynes was not the only economist to challenge the orthodoxy of the time, and the *General Theory* was not the only important work to do so. As Hayek wrote in a slightly different context: "We all had similar ideas in the 1920's." [7] Leijonhufvud pointed out that to describe the *General Theory* as a "clean break" is to miss the clear progression from the ideas of the *Treatise*.[8]

A major premise of this work is that Hayek was correct in his contention that the ideas that bore fruit in the late depression period were conceived in the boom of the twenties. I shall reexamine the contribution of Hayek to this period of intense questioning of economic orthodoxy, especially in relation to the problem of the business cycle in a decentralized market economy.

THE PROBLEM IN PERSPECTIVE

Even before Hayek was awarded the Nobel Prize there was a revival of interest in his contributions to economics. Some credit for this revival belongs to Hicks, though he only examined Hayek's works dealing directly with business cycle theory (and erred in ignoring the analysis of the price mechanism as an information–transmitting device in a decentralized market economy). To Hayek, the price system, by disseminating available information to market participants at the least cost, tended to make mutually compatible the initially incompatible plans of individual actors in that system. His work forms a unified whole and must be appreciated as such.

It is impossible to assess adequately Hayek's business cycle theory, as Hicks attempted, without considering his work on the foundations of economic theory and the operation of the price system. Hayek's conception of how the market economy operates is most evident in his theoretical work about prices as transmitters of information. Even the contributors to the recent *Festschrift* honoring Hayek did not attempt such a reintegration.[9]

G. L. S. Shackle summarized the prevailing view of economists during the 1920s that their science was the "human counterpart of celestial mechanics." According to Shackle, a "Grand System of Economics," an orthodoxy, emerged after 1870. Economics became a theory of "general, perfectly competitive, full–employment stationary (or better, timeless) equilibrium." It was an economics in which, for instance, the existence of money made little sense.[10]

I consider Hayek's work a radical criticism of the "Grand System" concept of economics. In presenting an overview of the state of economic theory during the 1920s, it is necessary to contrast the economic theory prevailing in Great Britain (and, to some extent, the United States) with that on the Continent. Shackle's description of economics during the 1920s is more applicable to British classical economics (as modified by William Stanley Jevons, Alfred Marshall, A. C. Pigou, and others) than it is to Continental economics.

According to most histories of economic thought, the writings of the three "discoverers" of the doctrine of marginal utility (that is, Jevons, Léon Walras, and Carl Menger) are essentially the same. The contributions of each were synthesized by Marshall with what was worthwhile in classical economics. For a variety of reasons, the Marshallian system was replaced with the Hicks–Samuelson, neo–Walrasian, general equilibrium approach. The "new" microeconomics was eventually blended with Keynesian macroeconomics, and the resulting core of economic theory is described as the "neoclassical synthesis." This is clearly a solecism: a more accurate description of current economics would be neo-neoclassical. The neo-neoclassical economists were Jevons, Walras, Menger, and their followers. To insist that contemporary orthodox economics is founded on early marginalism is to minimize the influence of Hicks and Paul Samuelson and, by implication, to deny the revolutionary character of Keynes's work.

This textbook view of economic thought is not only semantically inaccurate but also errs in claiming to capture the common denominator of the works by Jevons, Walras, and Menger. In effect the textbook approach emphasizes the conceptual similarities among these economists rather than the areas of disagreement. I maintain that the Marginal Revolution had three distinct phases, each developing along dissimilar lines in the twentieth century.[11] Indeed, the history of twentieth-century economic thought is best understood if the thesis of a unified neoclassical economics is rejected.[12]

In fact, regardless of one's attitude about the unity of neoclassical economics, it was the Austrian variant that dominated thinking on the Continent during the first half of this century. Thus Knut Wicksell wrote in 1924:

Menger . . . was successful in establishing a school of enthusiastic and highly talented followers, the Austrian School, whose doctrines spread over the whole world, and for a period of fifty years set the course of all work and discussion in theoretical economics, and to some extent in fiscal theory too.[13]

I would amend Wicksell by saying that Menger's doctrines spread over the whole non–Anglo–Saxon world. Throughout the 1920s English economists remained largely ignorant of the Austrian school.[14] On the Continent, however, economists in Germany, Austria, and Sweden communicated with one another, and a separate intellectual tradition developed. Swedish and Austrian economists in particular were doing original research on monetary theory, the business cycle, and dynamic equilibrium analysis.

Though there is undeniably a distinctly Austrian contribution, it is easier to specify aspects of this contribution than it is to determine what differentiated economists of the Austrian school from other economists. Hicks emphasized their unique contributions to capital theory and also Menger's important insights about the nature of money.[15] James Buchanan detailed the Austrian roots of the London School of Economics' tradition in cost theory—a tradition that consistently rejects the real cost doctrines that permeate many current discussions in economics.[16] But what, if anything, is peculiarly "Austrian"?

From the beginning, that is, from the publication of Carl Menger's *Grundsätze*, economists identifying with the Austrian school insisted on following two procedures in economics: first, they were strict methodological individualists, and, second, they faithfully avoided injecting normative judgments into positive economic analysis.[17] A by-product of their adherence to methodological individualism was their adoption of subjectivism as fundamental to explanation and discovery in economics.[18] Their original advocacy of a sharp distinction between positive and normative economics is now widely accepted, no longer being peculiar to Austrian economics (though few economists are aware of the Austrian influence in this area). To the extent that individual economists compromised the principles of subjectivism and methodological individualism they became less distinctively Austrian.

There is another characteristic of Austrian economics that distinguishes it from the Lausanne school in particular: Austrian contributions could not be subsumed into what Shackle described as the "Grand System" because they focused attention on the element of adjustment time and consequently adopted the causal–sequential analysis of classical economics rather than the technique of mutual determination.[19] This rejection of mutual determination has been taken as evidence that their intellectual contribution was outdated. Furthermore it has led to the spurious claim that they ignored the mutual interdependence of economic factors.[20] To the contrary, their approach was a by-product of a concern with market processes rather than equilibrium states, a concern that attained its fullest development in the writings of Mises and Hayek.[21] Many of the positions viewed as characteristically Austrian may be traced to the work of these

writers, whose work nonetheless represents the fullest development of this tradition.

Austrian and Swedish economists, familiar with the work of
Menger and his disciples, pioneered the technique of dynamic
analysis. Educated on the Continent, they, unlike their English
counterparts, were aware of the Walras–Pareto tradition, and its
limitations. Although the Swedish economists alone have been
credited with "process analysis," Hayek was working along similar lines at the same time. In essence, the Swedish and Austrian
economists were recasting economic theory so as to focus on the
market *process*, by which disparate plans of individuals are
equilibrated, rather than on equilibrium *states*.

In Sweden both Erik Lindahl and Gunnar Myrdal were refin-
ing the work of Wicksell; in Austria Mises and Hayek were
extending the work of Eugen von Böhm–Bawerk and Wicksell.
Thus in 1933 Hayek edited a work of non–German contributions, *Beitrage zür Geldtheorie* (Vienna, 1933), which contained
articles by both Wicksell and Myrdal. Myrdal's contribution,
"Der Gleichgewichtsbegriff als Instrument der Geldtheoret-
ischen Analyse," did not appear in English until 1939.[22]

Shackle argued for the simultaneity (if not the priority) of
Myrdal's "Keynesian" analysis with Keynes's own; indeed,
Shackle suggested that in some ways Myrdal's performance was
more satisfying than that of Keynes in *The General Theory*. He also
claimed priority for Myrdal in formulating and effectively
employing the *ex ante–ex post* distinction.[23] But as a matter of
priority in the history of thought, it is necessary to note the
independent work of Hayek here; though, again, the Swedish
and Austrian economists wrote under the common influence of
the early Austrians.[24]

Before the 1930s English economists were as ignorant of these
later Continental developments as they were of the earlier ones.
Hayek thus could say of Keynes's *Treatise* that it contained nothing new for a Continental economist (adding that the presentation was somewhat confusing). At the time of the *Treatise*, Keynes
was apparently unaware of Böhm–Bawerk's capital theory, a fact
Hayek underscored in his 1931 review of the work.[25]

In Shackle's "Grand System," economics deals with long-run phenomena. Whatever reasons economists may have had for couching their analyses in these terms, the result proved unsatisfactory for coping with the disequilibrium problems that increasingly occupied economists in the post–World War I period. It is to this set of short-run phenomena that I now turn.

HAYEK ON EQUILIBRIUM

Hayek argued that a successful analysis of economic disequilibrium required a reformulation of the concept of equilibrium. He devoted considerable energy to this task. Through the late 1930s and the 1940s he published articles on the price mechanism and the social function of prices in transmitting knowledge. From one viewpoint, these articles are a continuation of the debate about economic calculation in a Socialist economy. From another, these writings, together with his work on economic calculation and on monetary theory, attempt to come to grips on different levels with a single basic problem; for his price theory may be interpreted as an extension of his business cycle theory.[26] All Hayek's work may thus be seen as flowing from a conception of social interaction with emphasis on economic allocation.

Is it proper to assess Hayek's lifework as the logical development of a single idea? Although much of his work on monetary theory and the business cycle was written before that on price theory, my impression is that he was systematically working out the basic assumptions of his monetary theories in response to criticisms and misunderstandings.[27] On several occasions Hayek expressed surprise that his English readers were not familiar with areas of economic knowledge that to him were commonplace.

Schumpeter's insight that a man's work depends on his total conception of the economic problem is apropos.[28] Thus, the purpose of this work is to elucidate Hayek's conception of the market process. Among other things, this elucidation may assist in the reformulation of macroeconomics.

CHRONOLOGY OF WORKS

Prices and Production (for complete citations see bibliography at the end of this book) was Hayek's first major work in English. First published in 1931, *Prices and Production* brought Hayek widespread recognition in England and introduced the Austrian business cycle theory to the British. *Monetary Theory and the Trade Cycle* was not translated and published until 1933, though it appeared in German in 1928. Expressing, as it does, Hayek's views on monetary theory in more detail, *Monetary Theory and the Trade Cycle* should be read before *Prices and Production*. Yet English readers did not have access to the earlier work until two years after the publication of *Prices and Production*.

Hayek was a major participant in the Socialist calculation debate and edited a volume on the subject in 1935 entitled *Collectivist Economic Planning*. Concomitantly, he was presenting his monetary, capital, and business cycle theory in journals. These researches on the business cycle and on the Socialist calculation question suggested the need for a firmer foundation for price theory. Hayek believed that the crucial role of prices in resource allocation was not fully appreciated. In a series of articles written between 1936 and 1946, he emphasized that prices serve two important functions: They communicate information about the relative scarcity of resources, and under certain assumptions they improve coordination of the plans of transactors.[29]

The connection between Hayek's work on the price system and on resource allocation in a centrally planned economy is readily apparent. The connection that exists between work on monetary theory and on the theory of economic fluctuations may be less clear. However, Hayek saw the business cycle as resulting from the noncorrespondence of plans of savers and investors when important market signals—relative prices—are falsified by previous monetary disturbances.

Hayek restated his business cycle theory in 1939.[30] However, his *magnum opus* on capital theory, *The Pure Theory of Capital*, was not published until 1941. Again, this work elucidated the foundations for work that had been published years earlier.

In the 1940s Hayek turned his attention to other matters. He began working in the philosophy of science and the social sciences in general, on political philosophy, and on the theory of perception. Hayek confessed that by the 1950s he had lost interest in monetary theory.[31]

This book will end where Hayek's interests changed. It will thus examine only about half of his total output. But to examine that half, we have to read Hayek in logical rather than chronological order.

NOTES

1. Sir John Hicks, "The Hayek Story," *Critical Essays in Monetary Theory* (Oxford: Oxford University Press, The Clarendon Press, 1967), p. 203. (Hereafter, *Critical Essays*.)

2. Compare Thomas S. Kuhn, *The Structure of Scientific Revolution* (Chicago: University of Chicago Press, 1963); see also Axel Leijonhufvud, *On Keynesian Economics and the Economics of Keynes* (New York: Oxford University Press, 1968), pp. 5-6. (Hereafter, *Keynesian Economics*.)

3. On Keynes–versus–the–classics debate, see, for example, W. H. Hutt, *Keynesianism: Retrospect and Prospect* (Chicago: Henry Regnery Co., 1963); Robert Lekachman, *The Age of Keynes* (New York: Random House, 1967); Hicks, *Critical Essays*; J. Ronnie Davis, *The New Economics and the Old Economists* (Ames, Iowa: Iowa State University Press, 1971) (hereafter, *The New Economics*). On Keynes and the Keynesians, Axel Leijonhufvud, *Keynesian Economics*; Hershel I. Grossman, "Was Keynes a 'Keynesian'?" *Journal of Economic Literature* 10 (March 1972): 26-30; and G. L. S. Shackle, "Keynes and Today's Establishment in Economic Theory: A View," *Journal of Economic Literature* 11 (June 1973): 516-19.

4. This shift occurred once economists were confident that they understood Keynes's message.

5. See Davis, *The New Economics*, passim. See also idem, "Henry Simons, the Radical: Some Documentary Evidence," *History of Political Economy* 1 (Fall 1969): 388-94. Also relevant is the discussion in Leijonhufvud, *Keynesian Economics*, pp. 31-35.

6. Leijonhufvud, *Keynesian Economics*, pp. 24ff; 37-38; and passim. Yeager argued that Keynes cannot be easily credited with what Leijonhufvud claimed for him (cf. Leland Yeager, "The Keynesian Diversion," *Western Economic Journal* 11 [June 1973]: 150-63).

7. Hayek to Milton Friedman, commenting on the latter's Henry

Simons Lecture, wrote: "I believe you are wrong in suggesting the common element in the doctrine of Simons and Keynes was the influence of the Great Depression. We all held similar ideas in the 1920's. They had been more fully elaborated by R. G. Hawtrey who was all the time talking about the 'inherent instability of credit,' but he was by no means the only one. . . . It seems to me that all the elements of the theories which were applied to the Great Depression had been developed during the great enthusiasm for 'business cycle theory' which preceded it" (Milton Friedman, *The Optimum Quantity of Money* [Chicago: University of Chicago Press, 1969] p. 88n).

Not only was Hayek an active participant in these debates, but his consummate skill as a doctrine–historian and interpreter of economic theories is above dispute. For a compliment by a contemporary historian of the institutionalist school, whose section on Hayek can otherwise only be described as a series of misinterpretations and one-sided attacks, see Ben B. Seligman, *Main Currents in Modern Economics*, 3d ed. (New York: Free Press of Glencoe, 1963), pp. 342-43.

8. See Leijonhufvud for discussions of the continuity of Keynes's thought, for instance, the section on the relationship between the *Treatise* and the *General Theory* in Leijonhufvud, *Keynesian Economics*, pp. 15-31.

9. Erich Streissler et al., eds., *Roads to Freedom* (New York: Augustus M. Kelley, 1969); but see Ludwig M. Lachmann, "Methodological Individualism and the Market Economy," ibid., pp. 89-103.

10. G. L. S. Shackle, *The Years of High Theory* (Cambridge: Cambridge University Press, 1967), pp. 4-5. "Money is the refuge from specialized commitment, the postponer of the need to take far–reaching decisions." Yet in orthodox theory, money was but a "veil" (ibid., p. 6).

11. "Their 'common denominator' . . . has with time become uninteresting and an obstacle to clear thought. The common denominator goes under the label of the 'Marginalist Revolution'—portrayed as the simultaneous discovery of the first derivative of practically everything (followed, after decades of hard 'neoclassical' work, in due course by the discovery of the second derivative of absolutely everything). This is a conception of the work of the 'neoclassical' giants that irreparably trivializes their contributions in the eyes of a calculus–trained student generation" (Axel Leijonhufvud, "The Varieties of Price Theory: What Microfoundations for Macrotheory?" U.C.L.A. Discussion Paper no. 44 [Los Angeles: mimeographed 1974], 3); abbreviated, "Varieties of Price Theory." See also William Jaffé, "Menger, Jevons, and Walras De–Homogenized," *Economic Inquiry* 14 (December 1976): 511-24.

12. As an example, the paper by Leijonhufvud (see note 11), an outgrowth of his work on the microfoundations of macrotheory, demonstrated that there is "more than one 'variety of price theory'." This

insight indicates why economists have been remiss in providing needed microfoundations for macrotheory and why they have often found Keynes's own efforts in this regard confusing.

Leijonhufvud's "grand conclusion" lends support to my own argument: "Let us be done with the term 'neoclassical theory' " (Leijonhufvud, "Varieties of Price Theory," pp. 2, 47).

Mark Blaug noted that the so-called marginal revolution was composed of three distinct revolutions—"the marginal utility revolution in England and America, the subjectivist revolution in Austria, and the general equilibrium revolution in Switzerland and Italy" ("Was There a Marginal Revolution?" in *The Marginal Revolution in Economics*, ed. R. D. Collison Black, A. W. Coats, and Craufurd D. W. Goodwin [Durham: Duke University Press, 1973], p. 14).

13. Knut Wicksell, "The New Edition of Menger's *Grundsätze*," in *Selected Papers on Economic Theory*, ed. Erik Lindahl (London: George Allen & Unwin, 1958), p. 193.

14. It is true that Carl Menger and Eugen von Böhm–Bawerk were read to a limited extent in the United States. Jacob Viner for one was familiar with the general Austrian approach ("Cost Curves and Supply Curves," in *Readings in Price Theory*, ed. George J. Stigler and Kenneth Boulding [Homewood, Ill.: Richard D. Irwin, 1952], pp. 198-226, esp. p. 200). Developments in the United States were less important at this time. The Austrians remained largely unknown in Great Britain, and to a great extent, despite the translation of Böhm–Bawerk's work and the best efforts of men like Viner, Irving Fisher, and J. B. Clark, in the United States as well. It must be remembered that the *locus classicus* of the Austrian school, Menger's *Grundsätze*, was not translated until 1950 (Carl Menger, *Principles of Economics*, trans. and ed. James Dingwall and Bert F. Hoselitz [Glencoe, Ill.: The Free Press, 1950]).

Credit belongs to Lord Robbins for breaking down British intellectual insularity in the 1930s and bringing Continental developments to the attention of British economists. Hayek's invitation to lecture at the London School was a by–product of these efforts.

15. Hicks discussed Austrian capital theory in *Capital and Time* (Oxford: Oxford University Press, Clarendon Press, 1973). On Menger, see John R. Hicks, *Theory of Economic History* (New York: Oxford University Press, 1969), p. 63; see also Boris P. Pesek and Thomas R. Saving, *Money, Wealth, and Economic Theory* (New York: Macmillan Co., 1967), pp. 47-48, for an appreciation that includes Ludwig von Mises.

16. James Buchanan, *Cost and Choice* (Chicago: Markham Publishing Co., 1969).

17. Ironically, the latter–day Austrians (that is, Ludwig von Mises and those who attended his seminar at the University of Vienna, including Hayek, Fritz Machlup, and Oskar Morgenstern among the younger generation) saw themselves as members of the same school in

a geographical sense only. Otherwise, they considered themselves orthodox economists and applauded the demise of the Austrian school as
a distinct intellectual entity. Clearly I do not accept the view that they
then held; moreover, I think the course of history argues against their
view.

18. On the subjective nature of economics, see Hayek, *The Counter-
Revolution of Science* (New York: Free Press of Glencoe, 1955), pp. 25-35
and passim. See also Ludwig M. Lachmann, "Methodological Individualism and the Market Economy," in *Roads to Freedom*, ed. Streissler
et al., pp. 91-94.

19. Robert V. Eagly, *The Structure of Classical Economic Theory* (New
York: Oxford University Press, 1974), pp. 126-38. Menger noted that:
"The idea of causality . . . is inseparable from the idea of time. A process
of change involves a beginning and a becoming, and these are only
conceivable as processes in time. Hence it is certain that we can never
fully understand the causal interconnections of the various occur-
rences in a process, or the process itself, unless we view it in time and
apply the measure of time to it. Thus . . . time is an essential feature of
our observations" (*Principles of Economics* p. 67). He concluded this
section by discussing the significance of uncertainty in the process of
man producing in time. In Menger the clash with the static/general
equilibrium approach of Léon Walras is unequivocal. Erich Streissler
argued that "Menger's *Grundsätze* was an attempt to sketch a theory of
economic development" ("To What Extent Was the Austrian School
Marginalist?" in *Marginal Revolution*, ed. Black et al., p. 164).

20. George J. Stigler, *Production and Distribution Theories* (New York:
Macmillan Co., 1941), p. 181. For a strident attack on Stigler's position,
see Murray N. Rothbard, *Man, Economy, and State*, 2 vols. (Princeton:
D. Van Nostrand Co., 1962), 1: 279, 451n.

21. Lachmann, "Methodological Individualism," pp. 89-91.

22. Gunnar Myrdal, *Monetary Equilibrium* (London: William Hodge
& Co., 1939).

23. Shackle, *The Years of High Theory*, pp. 94-128. Shackle subsequently described Myrdal's achievement as providing a "language"
that renders Keynes's fundamental equations (in the *Treatise*) intelligible ("The 1974 Nobel Prize for Economics," *Science* 186 [Nov. 15,
1974]: 622).

24. An incorrect inference should not be drawn from the fact that
Hayek edited a volume in which Myrdal's now–famous essay appeared.
Hayek, wanting to make available in German those essays "which had
not been available in one of the generally understood languages,"
appealed to Lindahl. Lindahl was unable to supply Hayek with a new
work, and instead had his student Myrdal submit an essay. In no sense
then was Hayek influenced by Myrdal. And work that Hayek wrote
subsequently can be understood, it will be argued, entirely in terms of

his own earlier development. Hayek himself told me of the way in which Myrdal's piece came to be included in the volume in question; the information was conveyed in a letter dated 25 August 1974.

25. Friedrich A. Hayek, "Reflections on the Pure Theory of Money of Mr. J. M. Keynes," part 1, *Economica* 11 (August 1931): 277-80; J. M. Keynes, "A Reply to Dr. Hayek," ibid., 11 (November 1931): 394-95; Friedrich A. Hayek, "A Rejoinder," ibid., 11 (November 1931): 401-2; and idem, "Reflections," part 2, ibid., 12 (February 1932): 25-26.

26. Many of the essays on the price system were reprinted in *Individualism and Economic Order*. A series of articles in *Economica* in the 1940s on his philosophy of the social sciences are incorporated into *Counter-Revolution of Science*. Generally overlooked, these articles are basic to Hayek's approach to economics. The Socialist calculation debate concerned the possibility of allocating resources by central authority, i.e., without the aid of a price system.

27. For the chronology of Hayek's work, see pp. 10-11.

28. Schumpeter spoke of a man's "vision." He cited Keynes as the major example of the view that a man's work evolves from a basic insight (Joseph A. Schumpeter, *History of Economic Analysis* [New York: Oxford University Press, 1954], pp. 41-43).

29. The papers are "Economics and Knowledge" (1936), "The Use of Knowledge in Society" (1945), and "The Meaning of Competition" (1946); all are reprinted in *Individualism and Economic Order*.

30. "Profits, Interest, and Investment," in *Profits, Interest, and Investment* (New York: Augustus M. Kelley, 1970). Reprint of 1939 edition.

31. "Twenty years ago I lost interest in monetary matters because of my disillusionment with Bretton Woods. I was wrong in my prediction that the arrangement would soon disappear" (Sudha R. Shenoy, ed., *A Tiger by the Tail* [London: The Institute of Economic Affairs, 1972], p. 112).

2

The Coordination Problem

The proper field of economic study is, in the first instance, the type of relationship into which men spontaneously enter, when they find that they can best further their own purposes by approaching them indirectly (Philip H. Wicksteed, "The Scope and Method of Political Economy" [1914].)

THE PROBLEM TODAY

Progress in science occurs more slowly than many modern chroniclers would have us believe.[1] In economics the persistence of problems, for example, economic disequilibrium, makes progress an elusive goal. The theoretical problem here is twofold: first, the theory must be applicable to nonequilibrium situations, and second, a description must be offered of the behavior of transactors when the price and quantity variables have other than equilibrium values.

Thinking "Walrasianly" has not promoted progress here.[2] Robert Clower pointed out that neo–Walrasian theory has proved even less conducive to the integration of monetary and value theory.[3] The theoretical issues surrounding the business cycle (the practical economic problem after World War I as it had been after the Napoleonic Wars) are again in center stage. The question now, as then, is, "the extent to which the economy, or at least its market sectors, may properly be regarded as a self–regulating system." [4]

Whether and to what extent a market economy is a "self–regulating" system depends on the information available to transactors.[5] Disequilibrium is the result of less than perfect information. Neo–Walrasian economic theory is not concerned with other than equilibrium values for the endogenous variables.[6] In neo–Walrasian general equilibrium theory, there can be no information problems. Not unexpectedly, attempts to integrate monetary and value theory are aborted, inasmuch as the presence of money is an indication of uncertainty about the future.[7]

There is an uneasy alliance between microeconomics and macroeconomics, and "general economic theory [is] split down the middle." [8] The neo–Walrasian theory of price determination and the Keynesian theory of unemployment are united in what has been called "the Grand Neoclassical Synthesis." [9] That synthesis is a source of confusion for the teacher as well as the student of modern economics.[10]

During the interlude between the two World Wars, these same issues were debated, and out of this debate the current state of economic theory evolved. The fundamental issues were never resolved.

In this debate Hayek criticized both Marshallian economics (then dominant in Great Britain) and neo–Walrasian economics (to become dominant in Anglo-American economics). Hayek argued that neither of these orthodox paradigms gives adequate attention to the information problem inherent in economic activity.

In writings on the price system as a transmitter of information, Hayek developed a concept of equilibrium that referred to the *consistency* of the plans of transactors and to the *information* required to attain this consistency. Hayek also analyzed the problem of the allocation of resources over time. To some extent, Hayek set forth his conception of the role of prices to amplify his theory of the business cycle. Yet the relevance of his work on prices and markets to this theory of cyclical fluctuations has not been made explicit in the literature.

REVOLUTION AND COUNTERREVOLUTION IN ECONOMICS

The revolution against what G. L. S. Shackle called the "Grand System" was carried on by a number of protagonists including Keynes. The final victory was won by the counterrevolution effected by J. R. Hicks and Paul Samuelson. Robert Eisner spoke of the "neo–classical resurgence," which purged growth theory

of its Keynesian content.[11] Clower argued that the basic properties of neo–Walrasian general equilibrium theory rule out
Keynesian income constrained processes, because Walrasian
economics is concerned only with equilibrium states.[12]

Throughout the 1930s and 1940s, Hayek was a major critic of
the emerging professional consensus on economic research. In
particular, he tried to separate the theoretical from the empirical
(as he phrased it) in economics and delimit the tautological
propositions of economic analysis from the potentially empirical
elements. He argued that the tendency to limit economic theory
to the development of static analysis would make it impossible to
deal with disequilibrium conditions. His arguments often anticipated current criticisms of the cavalier treatment of disequilibrium states by economists.

Marshallian theory was dominant in Great Britain until the
1930s, particularly at Cambridge. However, iconoclasts and independent thinkers at the London School of Economics were
not enamored with Marshall. Lionel Robbins recorded a re-
sentment toward Cambridge for constantly arguing that "it's all
in Marshall!" Cambridge appeared almost impervious to
"foreign" intellectual influences, there being a general ignorance of developments in languages other than the "king's
tongue." [13]

Probably the London School's lack of a theoretical tradition
led to its becoming the locus for the introduction of Walrasian
(and Paretian) economics by Hicks, and of Austrian economics,
first by Lionel Robbins and later by Hayek. Interest in Walrasian
economics was revived amid the general upheaval in economics,
though many of the ideas were "in the air" earlier, especially at
the London School.[14] Hicks's revision in demand analysis has
had more far-reaching consequences than were foreseen at the
time.

Walras nowhere described the processes in an existing market; his theory of general equilibrium is a skeleton construction,
since his purpose was other than that of analyzing actual market
behavior. Marshall, on the other hand, retained the flavor of the
competitive market process. The procedure chosen by Walras is
not necessarily less acceptable than the one chosen by Marshall.
In projecting in a logically tight fashion (or in a "mathematical"

manner) the equilibrium conditions of a competitive system, Walras deliberately relied on a number of "fictions" (in part to prevent the production of "false quantities").[15] His summary references to the efficiency of the *Bourse* are more an expression of a *belief* in markets than an actual theory of markets and how they operate: a belief that markets react with sufficient rapidity that observed shortages and surpluses will be eliminated by a speedy adjustment in prices, and that nothing prevents the attainment of competitive equilibrium.[16]

To describe Hayek's views on the nature and character of formal theory as an attack on formal theory per se would be incorrect.[17] Walras necessarily streamlined his theoretical edifice. Given his purpose, problems of short-run market behavior were ignored.[18] Walras was not only an innovator in applying mathematical analysis to economic theory but also in introducing the concept of general equilibrium, along with a reconstruction of the entire classical edifice. The additional construction of a theory of disequilibria would have been more than could be reasonably expected in such a pioneering work.

Hayek believed that his contemporaries were not always in touch with the "fictions" and limitations inherent in general equilibrium theory and were prone to confuse statements about equilibrium with the theory of the approach to equilibrium.[19] To assert that it is *as if* "so and so is true" is not to construct a theory of what in fact *does* occur in markets. Indeed, the assertion may be a way to avoid analyzing the adjustment process in order to concentrate on another problem altogether.

HAYEK ON THE PURE LOGIC OF CHOICE

Hayek did not object to the use of mathematics in the development of formal economic theory. In fact he treated the pure theory of consumer choice as a basically logical system that would be particularly susceptible to mathematical formalization. He contended that the purpose of formalizing theory was sometimes forgotten:

My criticism of the recent tendencies to make economic theory more and more formal is not that they have gone too far but that they have not yet been carried far enough to complete the isolation of this branch of logic ["the Pure Logic of Choice"] and to restore to its rightful place the investigation of causal processes, using formal economic theory as a tool in the same way as mathematics.[20]

His objection was not to the progressive refinement of static theory but to "an excessive preoccupation with problems of the pure theory of stationary equilibrium." [21] This preoccupation was responsible for lack of attention to "causal processes" in the coordination of economic activity. Hayek's critique, though less strident and more succinct, was similar to Keynes's attack on A. C. Pigou. It is incorrect to assume that the actual market economy makes use of "logical implication" when "solving" problems in the context of general equilibrium analysis: "To assume all the knowledge to be given to a single mind in the same manner in which we assume it to be given to us as the explaining economists is to assume the problem away and to disregard everything that is important and significant in the real world." [22]

Any analysis of disequilibrium or of adjustment behavior involves the factor of anticipations. Interest in this subject in the 1920s and 1930s suggests a relationship between problems of incomplete information and disequilibrium and those of expectations. Two Americans, Irving Fisher and Frank H. Knight, laid the groundwork. Hayek, building on the work of his teacher Ludwig von Mises, brought their contributions as well as those of the Swedish economists Gunnar Myrdal and Erik Lindahl to the attention of both his German and his English readers.

The trend of economic theory did not carry over. After World War II interest in expectations faded. The factors of expectations and incomplete information were excluded from hypotheses. As a result, economic theory was devoid of much empirical content (and any Keynesian content); little consideration was given to the conditions under which equilibrium would be attained in the real world. This weakness in economic theory subsequently led Hayek into more detailed analysis of economic models (particularly that of perfect competition). Because the essential outlines of the (now) orthodox economic paradigm were already visible by the late 1930s, his critical analysis is especially relevant today.

As is now widely recognized, the theory of perfect competition ignores the adjustment process required to attain equilibrium. Nor does the theory guarantee the attainment of that state (in the absence of some remarkably stringent assumptions). The theory of perfect competition is restricted because it only defines equilibrium values. The conventional (that is, neo–Walrasian) theory of value and price may be termed equilibrium theory. Recent work has attempted to extend economic theory to dis-equilibrium situations.[23] Hayek's early diagnosis of the problem has been largely ignored. Yet consideration of his diagnosis would, on the one hand, have speeded the development of theories of market adjustment; and, on the other hand, it would have helped theorists avoid the intellectual dead-end of attempting to develop such theories basically within an equilibrium model.

Using the "competitive case" as an example Hayek considered the standard assumptions in economic theory:

1. Complete knowledge of the relevant facts on the part of all transactors in the market
2. Free entry—that is, the absence of restraints or artifically imposed costs on the movement of resources and prices
3. A homogeneous commodity being supplied and demanded by a large number of potential sellers and buyers, none of whom expects to affect prices to any extent[24]

Hayek commented on this approach as follows:

It will be obvious . . . that nothing is solved when we assume everybody to know everything and that the real problem is rather how it can be brought about that as much of the available knowledge as possible is used. This raises for a competitive society the question, not how we can 'find' the people who know best, but rather what institutional arrangements are necessary in order that the unknown persons who have knowledge suited to a particular task are most likely to be attracted to that task.[25]

The world that economists are ostensibly studying is that of the competitive process in motion. Yet the standard assumptions of price theory apply to the conclusion of this competitive process. While it is sometimes useful to assume that the economy is in long-run equilibrium, a study of the market process gets nowhere if the process is assumed to be finished. The key is the discovery of the institutional arrangements most likely to result in the wide dispersal of knowledge and free entry that is assumed to exist to begin with in the theory of competition.

The influence of Lionel Robbins's interpretation of economics as the science that studies the allocation of scarce means among competing ends cannot be overestimated, although he can scarcely be held responsible for the drift of economics subsequent to the publication of his *Essay*.[26] Yet in concentrating exclusively on Robbinsian maximizing behavior, economists have inhibited investigation into the market process.[27] According to Kirzner,

This analytical vision of economizing, maximizing, or efficiency–intent individual market participants is, in significant respects, misleadingly incomplete. It has led to a view of the market as made up of a multitude of economizing individuals, each making his decisions with respect to *given* series of ends and means. And in my opinion this view of the market is responsible for the harmful exclusive emphasis upon equilibrium situations. . . . A multitude of economizing individuals each choosing with respect to given ends and means cannot, without the introduction of further exogenous elements, generate a market process (which involves systematically *changing* series of means available to market participants).[28]

In this criticism, Kirzner followed Hayek's lead. Hayek concentrated on the first assumption in the theory of competition, that of perfect knowledge. In saying that knowledge of opportunities is "given," economists fail to specify *to whom* that knowledge is given.

As Hayek observed:

Datum means, of course, something given, but the question which is left open, and which in the social sciences is capable of two different answers, is to *whom* the facts are supposed to be given. Economists appear subconsciously always to have been somewhat uneasy about this point and to have reassured themselves against the feeling that they did not quite know to whom the facts were given by underlining the fact that they *were* given—even by using such pleonastic expressions as "given data." But this does not answer the question whether the facts referred to are supposed to be given to the observing economist or to the persons whose actions he wants to explain, and, if to the latter, whether it is assumed that the same facts are known to all the different persons in the system or whether the "data" for the different persons may be different.[29]

After invoking "perfect knowledge," economists then proceed to what is termed the "economic problem." All relevant information about alternatives, preferences, and the state of the arts are "known." The solution to this problem—the problem of allocating scarce but known means to (known) ends—is not an empirical one, but "purely one of logic. . . . The answer to the question . . . is implicit in our assumptions." [30] An analysis carried out with the aid of these assumptions produces expected consequences.

An important consideration here is the use of the term *equilibrium* in economics: "Taking the word 'equilibrium' in its usual sense to mean an 'absence of motion,' we shall say that *a market is in equilibrium if and only if market price and quantity traded are stationary over time*." [31] The informational structure is implicit in such treatments. For all markets to be in equilibrium implies that the plans of a multitude of disparate transactors are mutually compatible.[32] What then is the requirement for mutual compatibility of plans? According to Hayek, "It appears that the concept of equilibrium merely means that the foresight of the different members of the society is in a special sense correct." [33]

Complete and perfect foresight is most unlikely.[34] With decentralized decision making, each transactor must consider the *planned* actions of all other transactors on the basis of their information. It is not sufficient for an individual to have complete knowledge of all *objective* conditions (technology, resources, and so on). A subtle, though fundamental change has now occurred in the problem. What was originally assumed "given" to participants in the market was information about objective conditions—facts only available to the mind of each transactor—*and only those facts*. But complete knowledge is now seen to entail perfect foresight about what others will do given their limited information. Walrasian general equilibrium theory, while ostensibly about decentralized decision making, really only makes sense in the context of a single planner. The whole analysis is more applicable to a system of central planning than to a market economy. Hayek termed the change in the problem "insidious." The problem to be studied has been changed in a manner that maximizes the probability that no one will realize the "solution" is not a solution to the original problem, but to a new one altogether.[35]

Perfect knowledge means correct foresight. But, as Hayek put it:

Correct foresight is then not, as it has sometimes been understood, a precondition which must exist in order that equilibrium may be arrived at. It is rather the defining characteristic of a state of equilibrium.[36]

The attainment of equilibrium is a coordination problem. But the problem has been phrased in a question–begging manner:

The statement that, if people know everything, they are in equilibrium is true simply because that is how we define equilibrium. The assumption of a perfect market in this sense is just another way of saying that equilibrium exists but does not get us any nearer an explanation of when and how such a state will come about.[37]

Hayek's essays on the price system and markets are pro-legomena to any future study of economic systems and dynamic processes. They display an erudition and a depth of scholarship often lacking in works that admittedly make use of more modern research techniques. They show an appreciation of the economic problem as an ongoing social process. Furthermore these essays represent the theoretical foundation for Hayek's work on economic fluctuations and reveal the continuity of his thought in the area now divided into micro and macro economics. His conception of economics as the study of an interpersonal coordination problem is nowhere more evident than in his essays "Economics and Knowledge," "The Use of Knowledge in Society," and "The Meaning of Competition."[38]

STATIONARITY AND EQUILIBRIUM

Lurking behind the assumption of "given knowledge" is another one important for the model of perfect competition. That is the notion of stationarity. The assumption that the market can actually *attain* stationary equilibrium involves an additional empirical hypothesis concerning the extent of change occurring at any moment. In Hayek's "vision" of a developed economy, the businessman is constantly struggling to keep costs from exceeding prices in the face of continuously changing conditions. Hayek noted how

easy it is for an inefficient manager to dissipate the differentials on which profitability rests and that it is possible, with the same technical facilities, to produce with a great variety of costs are among the commonplaces of business experience which do not seem to be equally familiar in the study of the economist.[39]

In contrast with Hayek's view is the Schumpeterian one, in which recurring "clusters" of innovation require the attention of the entrepreneur from time to time. "Normal" conditions correspond to the usual construction of static equilibrium.[40]

Elaborating on his interpretation of the term *competition*, Hayek said that "competition is by its nature a dynamic process whose essential characteristics are assumed away by the assumptions underlying static analysis." [41] The reason the economist's construct of competition ends up meaning "the absence of all competitive activities," has to do with the assumption of stationarity.[42]

The assumption of stationary conditions, implicit or explicit, appears under a number of guises. Hayek attributed the widespread belief in the possibility of rational allocation without a functioning price system to this assumption.[43] Specifically, static cost theory is much less applicable to allocation problems than is usually supposed. The market process involves constant adjustment to ever–changing data; important information consists of the planned actions of *other* transactors. Costs are ephemeral, and profit is ever-present income.[44] Capital is seldom replaced by capital of the same type or of the same value. Returns to owners of existing capital are quasi–rents, and have no definite relation to market rates of interest except insofar as accounting procedures take account of implicit revaluations of assets. It is a world in which a "Lerner Rule" would be unusable.[45]

The alleged differences in the rates of return of industries of differing market concentration have been questioned. Some have asked whether the computed rates are merely "accounting" rates and without economic significance. Insufficient attention, however, has been paid to the cost-theoretic problem. Economists in practice either confuse a theoretical construct (i.e., general equilibrium) with a statement of fact, or they assume stationary conditions.[46]

Other difficulties in theory application result from presupposed stationary conditions.[47] But the point that will concern us is that it is impossible to transfer a stationary state or equilibrium view to a macroeconomic theory of short-run disequilibrium.

PRICES AND EQUILIBRIUM OVER TIME

The meaning of "equilibrium" can be understood with reference to the plans of a single transactor: his plans are mutually consistent.[48] But how is it that the plans of disparate, individual decision makers are made mutually consistent? Hayek proposed that we instead speak of a tendency for this compatibility to come about.[49] *"The division of knowledge"* is at least as important as "the division of labor," yet the former has been "completely neglected, although it seems to me to be the really central problem of economics as a social science."[50]

The problem which we pretend to solve is how the spontaneous interaction of a number of people, each possessing only bits of knowledge, brings about a state of affairs in which prices correspond to costs, etc., and which could be brought about by deliberate direction only by somebody who possessed the combined knowledge of all those individuals.[51]

The missing link in the chain of reasoning is the mechanism that tends to bring decisions into closer correspondence: the price system. Hayek, in a classic metaphor, suggested that "we must look at the price system as . . . a mechanism for communicating information if we want to understand its real function." [52] The price system is the mechanism to be focused on in a study of the coordination problem.

What particularly recommends the price system to Hayek is the "economy of knowledge" with which it operates. It is nothing short of a "marvel":

The marvel is that in a case like that of a scarcity of one raw material, without an order being issued, without more than perhaps a handful of people knowing the cause, tens of thousands of people whose identity could not be ascertained by months of investigation, are made to use the material or its products more sparingly; that is, they move in the right direction. This is enough of a marvel even if, in a constantly changing world, not all will hit it off so perfectly that their profit rates will always be maintained at the same even or "normal" level.[53]

The price system is a means of economically transmitting information among transactors: it produces information about changing market conditions.[54] The price system registers both the effects of changing objective conditions and the reactions of transactors to these changes. Most important, the price system is a mechanism—however imprecise—for registering the ever-changing expectations of market participants. What is important here is the argument that the price system is the cheapest possible system of resource allocation.

Prices are *inherently future oriented*, precisely because every action in the market place *ipso facto* involves an expectation. Action is impossible except in the context of time; all action must therefore involve the formation of *some* expectations.[55] Action is the execution of a plan. To argue (as some have) against the efficiency of a market system because it lacks future markets is surely to miss the point. If there are prices, the expectations of all market participants are thereby reflected for all others to interpret.[56]

Consistency of plans does not depend on a spurious assumption of stationarity. Rather one focuses on how well the mechanism functions, and to what degree, and in what manner transactors come to anticipate change. But before a meaningful analysis may be made of coordination mechanism failure, the circumstances under which the mechanism performs must be analyzed: "Before we can explain why people commit mistakes, we must first explain why they should ever be right." [57] Once it is realized that complete market coordination would involve complete knowledge by each actor of every other actor's plans, "imperfect" coordination is seen as an inevitable result of the fact that individuals differ. What remains to be explained by those enamored of such language is why the inevitable consequences of individual differences should be called "imperfections." Would a world in which we were all alike be perfection?

In the Socialist calculation debates, Hayek argued that the market system, with its relatively cheap communication network, is the best possible method of allocating resources. In his work on cyclical fluctuations, Hayek also focused on the coordination problem, this time to explain periodic breakdowns in a system that is *supposed* to work. Throughout all his work he maintained his conception of the "economic problem" as a coordination problem, for the analysis of which the method of "logical implication" is the appropriate tool.[58]

NOTES

1. See Imre Lakatos, "Methodology of Scientific Research Programmes," in *Criticism and the Growth of Knowledge*, ed. Imre Lakatos and Alan Musgrave (Cambridge: Cambridge University Press, 1970), pp. 174-75.

2. The term "Walrasianly" has been appropriated from J. R. Hicks, "A Neo–Austrian Growth Theory," *The Economic Journal* 89(June 1970): 257-58.

3. "Modern attempts to erect a general theory of money and prices on Walrasian foundations have produced a model of economic phenomena that is surprisingly reminiscent of the classical theory of a barter economy" (R. W. Clower, "Foundations of Monetary Theory," in *Monetary Theory*, ed. idem [Baltimore: Penguin Books, 1970], p. 202). Clower specifically referred to the works of Oskar Lange, Don Patinkin, J. R. Hicks, and Paul Samuelson. I have adopted "neo–Walrasian" to avoid doctrine-history squabbles.

4. Axel Leijonhufvud, "Effective Demand Failures," *Swedish Journal of Economics* 75 (1973):28. According to Leijonhufvud, the question has not been debated *explicitly* in this form. What he calls "the coordination problem" has always been the real issue.

5. Leijonhufvud, "Effective Demand Failures," pp. 37-41.

6. The problem considered by Leijonhufvud, whether the *form* of a model differs according to the values for the variables, is not considered at this point (Leijonhufvud, "Effective Demand Failures," p. 27).

7. See Shackle's remark on money in note 10 of the first chapter. Also see Murray N. Rothbard, "The Austrian Theory of Money," in *The Foundations of Modern Austrian Economics*, ed. Edwin G. Dolan (Kansas City: Sheed & Ward, 1976) pp. 171-72. Earl Thompson has suggested that while there may be perfect information in equilibrium in a model, there may not be perfect information in disequilibrium. His basic approach seems consistent with my argument (Earl Thompson, "The Theory of Money and Income Consistent with Orthodox Value Theory" [Los Angeles: mimeographed, 1972], p. 6).

8. Leijonhufvud, "Effective Demand Failures," p. 30.

9. Paul A. Samuelson, *Economics*, 6th ed. (New York: McGraw-Hill, 1964), pp. 360-61, 590.

10. "Despite the several alternative ways that we have developed to make the gulf between microtheory and macrotheory seem plausible to new generations of students, the micro–macro distinction remains basically that between models with 'perfectly coordinated' solutions and models where one or more markets reach such solutions only by chance. Both sets of exercises are referred to as 'theories,' but *there could be no real–world economy for which both are true at once*" (italics added) (Leijonhufvud, "Effective Demand Failures," 30-31). The addition of inconsistent hypotheses to an existing theoretical edifice does not necessarily involve methodological error. Lakatos argued that progress in the "hard" sciences has resulted from this procedure (*Criticism*, pp. 141-43). At some juncture, however, one "programme" has to go, or theoretical progress is halted.

11. Robert Eisner, "On Growth Models and the Neo–Classical Resurgence," *Economic Journal* 68 (December 1958): 707.

12. R. W. Clower, "The Keynesian Counter-Revolution: A Theoretical Appraisal," in *Monetary Theory*, ed. idem, pp. 270-97. Clower dates the counterrevolution to Hicks's article (p. 270). Eisner, on the other hand, dates the "retreat" from the fifties ("On Growth Models," p. 707).

13. On the milieu at Cambridge and at the London School of Economics, see Lord Robbins, *Autobiography of an Economist* (London: Macmillan & Co., 1971), pp. 105-6, 132-35. According to Hayek, Robbins played an important role in many of the developments that will be discussed.

14. Hicks noted that the concepts for *Value and Capital* were nurtured by what he termed a "sort of social process" at the London School in 1930-35. (John R. Hicks, *Value and Capital* [London: Oxford University Press, 1939], p. vi). Robbins discussed this social process in *Autobiography of an Economist*, pp. 129-32. Hicks and R. G. D. Allen referred to some of these concepts in "Reconsideration of the Theory of Value," *Economica*, n.s. 1 (February 1934): 52-76. There is irony in this story in that it was on Hayek's suggestion that Hicks investigated Pareto's indifference curve approach to demand theory. Hayek believed that Pareto's approach was in many ways superior to Marshall's (personal communication).

One can speculate why Hayek preferred Paretian over Marshallian demand theory. Paretian–Walrasian demand theory is more explicitly "choice–theoretic" and, thus, closer in spirit to the Austrian approach. On the distinction between Walrasian and Marshallian demand theory, see Leijonhufvud, "The Varieties of Price Theory: What Microfoundations for Macrotheory?" U.C.L.A. Discussion Paper No. 44 (Los Angeles: mimeographed, 1974).

15. Walras referred to his introduction of tickets (*bons*) as a "fiction" (Léon Walras, *Elements of Pure Economics*, trans. William Jaffé [New York: Augustus M. Kelley, 1969] p. 37). The classic discussion of Walras's problems with his *tâtonnement* process is in William Jaffé, "Walras' Theory of *Tâtonnement*: A Critique of Recent Interpretations," *Journal of Political Economy* 75(February 1967): 1-19.

16. Jaffé spoke of the "quasi–anecdotal" character of Walras's narrative about the *Bourse* (p. 4). Walras discussed the operation of the *Bourse* in the *Elements*, pp. 83-87. Walras's "faith" in markets is evident elsewhere (p. 106). Jaffé noted, specifically with reference to the *tâtonnement* process, that Walras had in mind "not a replica of the infinitely complex network of the heterogeneously organized markets of the real world, but a simplification of that network idealized in the sense that it was assumed to operate as a perfectly competitive mechanism" (pp. 11-12). Jaffé also suggested that Walras sought to lend "an air of empirical relevance to his abstract mathematical model of general equilibrium" (p. 2).

Clower and Due described Marshall's concept as "a more colorful and intuitively meaningful portrait of a market economy" than Walras's (Robert W. Clower and John F. Due, *Microeconomics*, 6th ed. [Homewood, Ill.: Richard D. Irwin, 1972], p. 24). At this point, Clower and Due were concerned with the treatment of money in the two paradigms.

There is some resemblance between Walras's *tâtonnement* process and auctions. An auction bid appears to be a *crie au hazard*. However, in actual auctions there are reservation prices of goods, and a given auction process depends on a past history of market prices and information, which usually have been arrived at by a method other than that of auctioning. Standard price theory does not allow for differences in actual market clearing prices depending on the selling methods chosen (for example, auction or "ordinary" market). Little work has been done on the relative efficiencies of various market forms. Yet in a world where transaction costs exist, the method of contracting could be very important (that is, there could be differential transactions costs in various market situations). Markets in the boom that characterized Western Europe from the eleventh century on were in the form of great fairs held several times a year in various localities, where goods of all descriptions would be bought and sold. The market form gradually evolved, however, until by the fourteenth century the fairs were unimportant except as clearing house mechanisms. On the role of such fairs in the medieval economy, see Henri Pirenne, *Economic and Social History of Medieval Europe* (New York: Harcourt, Brace & World, Harvest Books, 1933), passim. Pirenne attributed their decline to the guilds; the fairs inhibited the cartellization of crafts (pp. 209-10).

Steven N. S. Cheung has done a major part of the work on the efficiency of different market forms ("Transactions Cost, Risk Aversion, and the Choice of Contractual Arrangements," *Journal of Law and Economics* 12 [April 1969]: 23-42; idem, "The Structure of a Contract and the Theory of a Non-exclusive Resource," *Journal of Law and Economics* 13 [April 1970]: 49-70).

George J. Stigler presents the orthodox case against the form of market organization affecting equilibrium. Stigler ignores any transaction cost problem (*The Theory of Price*, 3d ed. [New York: Macmillan Co., 1966] pp. 94-95).

17. Here one should remember that Hayek is the author of *The Pure Theory of Capital* (Chicago: University of Chicago Press, 1941).

18. On Walras's precise task, see *Elements*, pp. 170, 241-42. Jaffé's assessment is that Walras failed in his objective to prove that the market's operation will result in the vector of prices and quantities being identical with the solution of his simultaneous equations.

19. Friedrich A. Hayek, "The Use of Knowledge in Society," in *Individualism and Economic Order* (Chicago: University of Chicago Press, 1948), pp. 89-91. (Hereafter, *Individualism*.)

20. Ibid., p. 35.

21. Hayek, "Socialist Calculation III: The Competitive Solution," *Individualism*, p. 188.

22. Hayek, "The Use of Knowledge in Society," p. 91. Walras seemed aware of the point Hayek made here (*Elements*, p. 106). See also J. M. Keynes, *The General Theory of Employment, Interest, and Money* (New York: Harcourt, Brace & World, 1936), pp. 272-79.

23. See, for example, K. J. Arrow, "Toward a Theory of Price Adjustment," in *The Allocation of Economic Resources*, ed. Moses Abram-

ovitz (Stanford: Stanford University Press, 1959), pp. 41-51; hereafter, "Toward a Theory." See also Israel M. Kirzner, *Competition and Entrepreneurship* (Chicago: University of Chicago Press, 1973); hereafter: *Competition*. Kirzner's work has an explicitly Hayekian (Austrian) framework; Arrow's has a neo–Walrasian equilibrium framework.

24. Hayek, "The Meaning of Competition," *Individualism*, p. 95. See also George J. Stigler, *The Organization of Industry* (Homewood, Ill.: Richard D. Irwin, 1968), pp. 5-16.

25. Hayek, "The Meaning of Competition," p. 95.

26. Lionel Robbins, *An Essay on the Nature and Significance of Economic Science*, 2d ed. (London: Macmillan & Co., 1935). "The book [i.e., Robbins's] has been so influential that its once challenging thesis will seem almost platitudinous to today's students. For that very reason, it should be recognized as an important part of the story of how choice-theory became the predominant—indeed, all but exclusive—paradigm of modern theoretical economics" (Leijonhufvud, "Varieties of Price Theory", 53n). Hayek convinced me that Robbins, in turn, was heavily influenced by the Austrian Richard von Strigl. Thus the earlier Austrians in part contributed to the development of a theoretical edifice they later came to reject.

27. The phrase "Robbinsian maximizing behavior" is Kirzner's (*Competition*, pp. 32-37).

28. Ibid., pp. 32-33.

29. Hayek, "Economics and Knowledge," *Individualism*, p. 39. Modern work on the technical issues involved in alternative assumptions about the dispersal of knowledge among economic actors, although accomplished within a neo–Walrasian framework, is of interest to the theorist. See Leonid Hurwicz, "The Design of Mechanisms for Resource Allocation," *American Economic Review* 63 (May 1973): 1-30.

30. Hayek, "The Use of Knowledge in Society," p. 77.

31. Clower and Due, *Microeconomics*, p. 52 (emphasis in original).

32. This section is based substantially on Hayek, "Economics and Knowledge," pp. 33-56, esp. pp. 35-45.

33. Ibid., p. 42.

34. It might be likely if the third assumption were true and we were dealing with an essentially stationary world. This possibility led Hayek to wonder whether the third assumption might imply the first.

35. Hayek, "Economics and Knowledge." pp. 38-39.

36. Ibid., p. 42.

37. Ibid., p. 46.

38. Among his writings on cycles and monetary theory the one entitled "Price Expectations, Monetary Disturbances, and Malinvestments" most clearly makes use of this conception, in *Profits, Interest, and Investment* (New York: Augustus M. Kelley, 1970), pp. 135-56. Signifi-

cantly, that essay antedates the three aforementioned essays on the price system.

39. Hayek, "The Use of Knowledge in Society," p. 82.

40. This could be overdrawn, of course, but there are differences. Stigler's view is essentially different from Hayek's": "These terms ['stable' and 'equilibrium'] were obviously borrowed from physics—has the economist made sure that they really make sense in economics? The answer is, let us hope, yes. The stability of equilibrium is indeed the normal state of affairs in a tolerably stable world" (*Theory of Price*, p. 93). For further elaborations on the differences between the Austrian and the Schumpeterian conceptions of the entrepreneur, see Kirzner, *Competition*; Rothbard, *Man, Economy, and State*, 2 vols. (Princeton: D. Van Nostrand Co., 1962), 2: 493-94.

41. Hayek, "The Meaning of Competition," p. 94.

42. Ibid., p. 96.

43. Much of Hayek's work on resource allocation was developed in the context of the Socialist calculation debates (Friedrich A. Hayek, ed., *Collectivist Economic Planning* [London: George Routledge & Sons, 1935]).

44. "Profits are a permanent income flowing from ever–changing sources, like the profits of a restaurant in which a different set of customers chooses a different set of dishes from the menu card every day" (Ludwig M. Lachmann, *Macro-economic Thinking and the Market Economy*, Hobart Paper No. 56 [London: Institute of Economic Affairs, 1973], p. 31). Buchanan most ably demonstrated that costs are an *unrealized* (and hence immeasurable) alternative (*Cost and Choice* [Chicago: Markham Publishing Co., 1969], pp. vii-x; and 38-50).

45. "To make a monopolist charge the price that would rule under competition, or a price that is equal to the necessary cost, is impossible, because the competitive or necessary cost cannot be known unless there is competition" (Hayek, "Socialist Calculation II: *The State of the Debate* (1935)," *Individualism*, p. 170).

46. One assumes that practitioners are not unaware of the theoretical problem and have a gestalt conception of markets significantly different from Hayek's. For sources on concentration and rates of return, see John S. McGee, *In Defense of Industrial Concentration* (New York: Praeger Publishers, 1971), p. 151n. For a criticism of the approach of many of these statistical studies, see Yale M. Brozen, "The Antitrust Task Force Deconcentration Recommendation," *Journal of Law and Economics* 13(October 1970): 279-92.

47. Arrow pointed out that market adjustment behavior is often confused with long–run monopolistic power, a confusion that is elementary but widespread ("Toward a Theory," pp. 45-47).

48. Hayek, "Economics and Knowledge," pp. 35-37.

49. "It is only by this assertion that such a tendency [toward equilib-

rium] exists that economics ceases to be an exercise in pure logic and becomes an empirical science" (ibid., p. 44).

50. Ibid., p. 50.

51. Ibid., pp. 50-51.

52. Hayek, "The Use of Knowledge in Society," p. 86.

53. Ibid., p. 87. His *gestalt* conception is evident in this passage; parameters change so often that, before the transactor can execute his plans, he is compelled to revise them.

54. Hirshleifer, while acknowledging the "pioneering" quality of "The Use of Knowledge in Society," surely misinterprets the central message. The article is about the use *and* production of information ("Where Are We Now in the Theory of Information?" *American Economic Review* 63 [May 1973]: 34).

55. Hayek's mentor, Mises, was even more explicit on this point: "Action is always speculation. . . . In any real and living economy every actor is always an entrepreneur and speculator" (Ludwig von Mises, *Human Action* [New Haven: Yale University Press, 1949], p. 253).

56. The more finely developed the market for a commodity, the more accurately prices reflect anticipations and the better founded are anticipations. But the absence of an explicitly time–dated market for a commodity is one with the absence of opera in central Iowa: the division of labor is limited by the scarcity of means.

57. Hayek, "Economics and Knowledge," p. 34.

58. Austrian economists have been viewed as unremitting critics of the use of mathematics in economic theory. What *in fact* Hayek objected to about this tool in analyzing allocation questions was the assumption that a transactor's knowledge is necessarily consistent with the facts, and with each other's plans (Hayek, "The Use of Knowledge in Society," pp. 89-91).

3

The Monetary Theory

Mr. Locke. . . . has clearly seen that the abundance of money makes everything dear, but he has not considered how it does so. The great difficulty of this question consists in knowing in what way and in what proportion the increase of money raises prices (Richard Cantillon, *Essai sur la nature du commerce en général* [1755]).

MONETARY THEORY AND THE NEO-QUANTITY THEORY

Many of the lively monetary debates of the 1920s and 1930s concerned which issues come under the purview of monetary theory and what constitutes an adequate monetary explanation of cyclical fluctuations. To make sense of these debates, we must consider the differences between the conception of monetary theory then and now.

Many of the participants in the early debates had a wider conception of monetary theory than do contemporary monetary theorists. This narrowing of interests among monetary theorists is partly attributable to the Keynesian revolution. After Keynes there was a loss of interest in monetary theory as a separate field of inquiry. To some extent, the Keynesian interpretation of the liquidity trap and other passages in the *General Theory* cast doubt on the effectiveness of monetary policy altogether.[1] Similarly, research waned in related areas, such as business cycle theory, in which monetary theorists had always taken an active interest.

However, according to Harry Johnson, activity in monetary theory was again flourishing by 1962.[2] Increasing attention was paid to the work of the new monetary theorists. These theorists restricted their inquiry to three broad but interrelated areas: analysis of the demand for money, determination of the money stock (or the money supply function), and determination of aggregate nominal income.[3] Other important issues, such as

those raised by the Patinkin debate having to do with the long–
run neutrality of money, were generally abandoned.[4]

Milton Friedman's 1956 paper on the restatement of the quantity theory was a milestone in the revival of interest in monetary
theory.[5] His formulation of the quantity theory is one that has
greatly influenced the course of subsequent research. By in
effect redefining the scope of monetary theory, he has success-
fully focused attention on a narrow range of issues in monetary
theory and promoted the neglect of others.[6]

Friedman expressed his conception of the quantity theory as
follows: "The quantity theory is in the first instance a theory of
the *demand* for money. It is not a theory of output, or of money
income, or of the price level." [7] As he noted: "In order to have a
complete model for the determination of money income, it
would be necessary to specify the determinants of the structure
of interest rates, of real income, and of the path of adjustment in
the price level." [8] But if interest rates and real income are determined by forces other than the demand and supply for money,
then Friedman's restatement yields a theory of the equilibrium
level of money income despite his original disclaimer.[9]

In successive restatements of his original thesis, Friedman
consistently treated the determination of nominal income (in the
short run) as the chief goal of monetary theory.[10] Moreover, the
analysis of fluctuations in nominal income is carried out in terms
of the effects of an excess demand for money.[11]

Critics of the neo–quantity theory often seem reluctant to call
themselves "monetary theorists." The tendency is to accept a
neo–quantity theory explanation as *the* monetary explanation.
Contemporary opponents of monetarists find themselves in a
quandary as to what to call themselves.[12] Formal definitions of
monetary theory also reflect this change.[13]

Actually, monetarists are following Hicks's famous "Suggestion for Simplifying the Theory of Money." [14] It could be argued
that Hicks's suggestions are responsible for the change in
monetary theory. But, as is often true of novel ideas, implemen-
tation of Hicks's approach was slow.

Is there more to monetary theory than demand–and–supply
analysis of money, or the determination of nominal income? In

the post–World War I era monetary theory (specifically, the quantity theory) was criticized for overemphasizing the effects of an excess demand for money. According to Hayek and others, important phenomena were ignored if economists failed to significantly modify the analysis of the quantity theory, particularly in studying short-run economic fluctuations.

A historical background is essential for an understanding of the quantity theory as it appeared to monetary theorists in the early part of this century. Hayek's criticism of the quantity theory becomes meaningful once the character of the older quantity theory is properly delineated. And to the degree that the neo–quantity theory has kept essential features of the older quantity theory, Hayek's criticisms have more relevance today.

Hayek constructed his monetary theory upon the foundations laid by early British monetary theorists and Knut Wicksell and Ludwig von Mises. The specifically short-run character of Hayek's monetary analysis is significant, as is his use of the concept of the "neutrality of money." Let us now turn our attention to this development, and to monetary theory as it was at the beginning of the century.

THE QUANTITY THEORY

At the end of the nineteenth century Wicksell concluded that the quantity theory was the only "specific" theory of money available. What was specific about it for Wicksell was the *proportionality* theorem—the unique relationship between the stock of money and the purchasing power of a single unit of money—which held that price changes are ultimately in direct proportion to changes in the quantity of money:

Since, however, it is true of all commodities than [sic] an increase in supply in itself tends to lower their exchange value, there is nothing unusual in the quantity theory nor anything peculiar in money as such. The special peculiarity of the Quantity Theory consists in the proportionality required between the quantity of money and commodity prices.[15]

Thus, Wicksell argued that "the whole dispute" over the quantity theory "turns ultimately on . . . whether the velocity of circulation of money is of autonomous or merely subordinate significance for the currency system."[16] But regardless of the outcome of this dispute, it was the quantity theorists alone who had something approximating a systematic theory. He believed the quantity theory to be basically correct for an inflow of specie, the case for which it was first developed. However, Wicksell thought it needed to be supplemented when dealing with the phenomena of an increase in the money supply in the form of bank credit.

Imprecision and lack of focus often characterize discussions of what the quantity theory is. Viewed as a *ceteris paribus* proposition the proportionality theorem is but a verbal presentation of the information in the equation of exchange: $MV = PQ$. I doubt whether quantity theorists ever intend *only* to assert this tautologous proposition.[17] While Wicksell suggested that the dispute over the validity of the quantity theory hinges on the question whether or not velocity is autonomous, Joseph Schumpeter, writing half a century later, suggested that the quantity theory should be defined in terms of four propositions: (1) that the quantity of money is autonomous with respect to prices and the physical volume of transactions; (2) that velocity is autonomous with respect to prices and the volume of transactions;[18] (3) that real output is unrelated to the quantity of money; and (4) that, *ceteris paribus*, variations in the quantity of money "act mechanically on prices," irrespective of the manner in which the variations first occur.[19]

According to Schumpeter, the only "major writers" to advance this extreme form of the quantity theory were John Wheatley, David Ricardo, James Mill, and John R. McCulloch.[20] Schumpeter here offered a more precise statement of the assumptions behind what Wicksell termed the proportionality theorem.

Wicksell cited few writers in his study. He relied mostly on Ricardo and J. S. Mill for statements of the proportionality version of the quantity theory. In the chapter "Of the Value of Money, as Dependent on Demand and Supply" in the *Principles*, Mill provided a straightforward account of the quantity theory.[21] Mill started with the case of "the arrival of a foreigner in a place, with a treasure of gold and silver." [22] Prices eventually rise uniformly: "Prices would have risen in a certain ratio, and the value of money would have fallen in the same ratio." The reader is told that "this ratio would be precisely that in which the quantity of money had been increased." [23] The teachings of Ricardo and James Mill are evident in John Stuart Mill's work a generation later. But too much had taken place in the intervening years for the younger Mill to let the subject rest there. When he considered the effects of credit, he amended his previous analysis:

The proposition which we have laid down respecting the dependence of general prices upon the quantity of money in circulation, must be understood as applying only to a state of things in which money, that is, gold or silver, is the exclusive instrument of exchange, and actually passes from hand to hand at every purchase, credit in any of its shapes being unknown. When credit comes into play as a means of purchasing, distinct from money in hand, we shall hereafter find that the connexion between prices and the amount of the circulating medium is much less distinct and intimate, and that such a connexion as does exist no longer admits of so simple a mode of expression.[24]

He concluded that the "sequel of our investigation will point out many qualifications . . . qualifications which, under a complex system of credit like that existing in England, render the proposition an extremely incorrect expression of the fact." [25]

Mill stated, in effect, what he thought was a necessary condition for the proportionality theorem to be applicable: the absence of bank credit. Once he introduced bank credit, he de-emphasized the mechanical linkage between a given change in the quantity of money and any subsequent change in prices.[26] Thus, in order to attribute a proportionality theorem to J. S. Mill, his observations on the determination of the "value of money" must be taken out of context.[27]

Let us grant, however, if not Mill then at least Ricardo was a genuine proponent of the quantity theory as defined by Wicksell and Schumpeter.[28] J. S. Mill's analysis of the "value of money," as determined by demand and supply, gave exposure to the quantity theory in the form of a proportionality theorem. But the result is curious: the strict quantity theory in the form of the proportionality theorem was severely criticized by J. S. Mill. Given Mill's position in economics, this should have been sufficient to bury the theory for at least fifty years. A lot of energy has been spent on a theory that by the middle of the nineteenth century had been rendered untenable—at least when stated in an unqualified form.

There is, however, another way to approach the controversy over the quantity theory—an approach that makes some sense out of this seemingly senseless dispute. Ricardo and his intellectual disciples were chiefly concerned with establishing comparative static propositions. The legacy of Adam Smith's treatment of the long run is evident in subsequent work. The long run, or *natural price*, "is, as it were, the central price, to which all the prices of all commodities are continually gravitating." [29] But a country blessed by wise rulers, just laws, and fortuitous circumstances might resist for long periods this central tendency. This resistance is accomplished by growth, which in this context means population growth and the accumulation of capital. The accumulation of capital in turn keeps the labor market in permanent disequilibrium and maintains wage rates above their long-run level.[30] But it was a "golden rule" of growth over time that occupied the later classical economists (especially the Ricardians), not the disturbing fluctuations around this trend.[31]

In all situations Ricardians in particular focused on the *ultimate* effects of a given change.[32] It was just this emphasis in classical economics to which Wicksell objected. Wicksell initially characterized the debate over the quantity theory as essentially a question of feedback effects on velocity of changes in the money stock, or the volume of transactions. The debate has traditionally been treated in this way.

But for some critics of the quantity theory the important issue is the *focus* of monetary theory—the ultimate effects of an increase of money on prices, or the process by which these changes occur. For Ricardo, the quantity theory was a tool to answer a specific question: what would be the results of a long period of increase in the quantity of banknotes? Ricardo treated the question as one of value theory and hence employed equilibrium analysis.[33] However, Henry Thornton, a contemporary of Ricardo's, wished to examine the process of adjustment to disequilibrium specifically in the loan market. Those who adopted this approach often focused on the effects of an increase in the quantity of money on borrowing and lending because the initial effects of a monetary disturbance are felt here. Quantity theorists, having adopted Ricardian thinking in monetary matters, focused on the increased spending in all markets (including the loan market) that *eventually* results. Thus quantity theorists asked whether prices will *eventually* rise uniformly as the result of a permanent change in the stock of money. Critics of the quantity theory approach were critical of the comparative static approach used in analyzing what are essentially disequilibrium situations. Beginning with Thornton and Malthus the critics focused on the loan market, for it was in the loan market that the new money entered the system.[34]

Malthus and Thornton made much the same point that the eighteenth–century critic Richard Cantillon made against John Locke's early formulation of the quantity theory.

He [Locke] realised well that the abundance of money makes everything dear, but he did not analyse how that takes place. The great difficulty of this analysis consists in discovering by what path and in what proportion the increase of money raises the price of things.[35]

Ricardo endorsed the cruder formulations of Locke and Hume as against the more refined analysis of Cantillon and Thornton. Successive generations reaffirmed the quantity theory, without perceiving how naked it was without a supporting theory of the short-run adjustment process.

To some critics, the crux of the quantity theory debate is the matter of velocity. However, few theorists subscribed to the view that velocity is constant, or that changes in the quantity of money automatically effect changes in prices. The differences among monetary theorists must lie elsewhere.

"Quantity theorists" such as Hume, Ricardo, and J. S. Mill analyzed the impact of a change in the quantity of money on actual and desired cash balances. Even when the impact of credit was considered, as in J. S. Mill's analysis, it was treated only insofar as it affected spending in general.[36] Thus, later quantity theorists analyzed monetary disturbances in terms of *aggregate* purchasing power and *aggregate* spending.

Any impact of changes in the supply of money or credit on the economy were regarded by quantity theorists as affecting spending directly. Henry Thornton is an example of someone who should *not* be classified as a "quantity theorist" because he did *not* conduct his monetary analysis in terms of the demand and supply of a subset of assets called "money." In fact, Thornton's specific contribution to monetary economics, aside from his criticism of the "real bills" doctrine, was his analysis of the indirect mechanism by which a monetary disturbance affects real economic activity. J. S. Mill started his monetary analysis by supposing "that to every pound, or shilling, or penny, in the possession of any one, another pound, shilling, or penny, were suddenly added." [37] Thornton, however, focused on monetary disturbance in capital markets and emphasized the gradual effects on spending by way of changes in the interest rates on marketable securities. "In order to ascertain how far the desire of obtaining loans at the bank may be expected at any time to be carried, we must enquire into the subject of the quantum of profit likely to be derived from borrowing there under the existing circumstances." [38]

The chief difference between Thornton and the "quantity theorists" is that the latter adopted the Ricardian approach of analyzing the long-run effects of a disturbance.[39] Thornton, on the other hand, was interested in the initial impact of a disturbance and the mechanisms effecting the ultimate outcome.[40]

Schumpeter's comparative evaluation of Ricardo and Thornton in monetary economics is appropriate:

In matters of monetary as of general theory, Ricardian teaching is a detour and . . . slowed up the advance of analysis, which could have been much quicker and smoother had Thornton's lead been followed—had Ricardo's force not prevailed over Thornton's insight.[41]

In Wicksell's initial analysis of the quantity theory the important question was the autonomy of velocity. But, as we shall emphasize in the next section, his emphasis in fact was, like Thornton's, on the transmission mechanism by which newly created money makes its way through the economy. Schumpeter, as already noted, presented four propositions to define the quantity theory.[42] His second proposition was the velocity is autonomous with respect to prices and the volume of transactions. However, Schumpeter, in his fourth proposition, pointed out that the manner in which money is introduced into the system is not important. The quantity theorist insofar as he is a Ricardian is concerned only with the long-run effects of a monetary disturbance. Thus *the quantity theory approach* is an analysis in which the long-run effects of a monetary disturbance are the main concern, to which short-run effects are incidental.[43]

The business cycle was not the major policy problem to nineteenth-century classical economists. Economic growth and development was the prime policy concern.[44] In classical analysis the quantity of money was unrelated to economic growth. The quantity of money in particular did not enter into the determination of the rate of interest and, hence, did not alter the rate of capital accumulation. Short-run effects of changes in the quantity of money were unimportant in the long run.[45]

The quantity theorist, then, focuses on the long-run effects of a monetary disturbance.[46] Although short-run effects are considered, the general tone of the analysis is to deemphasize them.[47]

It was against the quantity theory approach as described here that Wicksell and Hayek reacted. Their attitudes reflected the shift in emphasis from the study of economic growth to the study of cyclical fluctuations.

THE CHAIN CONNECTING MONEY AND PRICES

The theory Wicksell presented was not original though apparently he did develop it independently of other influences. There was a British tradition in monetary theory that sometimes paralleled and sometimes diverged from, but was quite independent of, Ricardo's quantity theory. In this respect, Wicksell's failure to mention Henry Thornton is perhaps the most striking *lacuna* in the *Lectures*.[48] Yet much of Wicksell's analysis of the interaction of money, credit, the interest rate, and prices duplicated Thornton's.

In his Introduction to Wicksell's *Lectures*, Lionel Robbins pointed out Wicksell's ignorance of this earlier tradition in British monetary theory. Wicksell apparently did not know of this tradition, save as it was embodied in a passage in Ricardo's *High Price of Bullion*, with which he became acquainted only after publication of his own work:

> I do not dispute, that if the Bank were to bring a large additional sum of notes into the market, and offer them on loan, but that they would for a time affect the rate of interest. The same effects would follow from the discovery of a hidden treasure of gold or silver coin. . . . It is only during the interval of the issues of the Banks, and their effect on prices, that we should be sensible of an abundance of money; interest would, during the interval, be under its natural level; but as soon as the additional sum of notes or of money became absorbed in the general circulation, the rate of interest would be as high.[49]

Ricardo's thesis is most uncanny in light of later developments. Yet he did not develop this short-run analysis any further.

Wicksell would not have learned about Henry Thornton's work through J. S. Mill's *Principles*. Though J. S. Mill cited Thornton extensively he did so only regarding the real-bills doctrine, and Mill completely ignored Thornton's analysis of the effects of changes in the money stock ("paper credit") on interest rates.[50]

To find "the right solution in this chaos of vague conceptions," Wicksell started his analysis–much as had Henry Thornton–by examining the effects of a monetary disturbance on market rates of interest.[51] The important question now is *how* more money enters the system. A lowering of market interest rates by an injection of money in the form of bank credit leads to increased investment. Changes in the demand–and–supply condition in commodity markets must then follow and thus changes in *com-*

position of output. A larger fraction of national income is devoted to investment expenditures, and as a result the marginal productivity of investment declines.[52]

Wicksell did not completely separate this theory from the quantity theory in the *Lectures*. Even though his real contribution was to analyze the effects of monetary disturbances on relative prices, he did not carry it through to a final conclusion.[53]

The history of twentieth–century monetary theory cannot be told without consideration of the Ludwig von Mises's *Theorie des Geldes und der Umlaufsmittel*, a major yet neglected work of this century.[54] Building on Menger, Mises was the first to integrate monetary theory into general economic theory using marginal utility analysis. His work was a textbook on the Continent, though it was unknown in Great Britain before the translation under the title *The Theory of Money and Credit*.[55]

In an odd way the success of Mises's work hurt it. As Robbins noted, the ideas worked their way slowly into Anglo–Saxon monetary theory, despite the wide currency of his ideas on the Continent. By the 1930s English–speaking economists could no longer recognize the revolutionary character of *The Theory of Money and Credit*.[56]

Mises extended the Wicksellian theory by explicitly examining the differential impact on demand for consumption and capital goods brought about by a divergence between loan and natural interest rates. Most important, he distinguished between the effects on general and relative prices. But his business cycle theory is marred by the manner of presentation. Much of *The Theory of Money and Credit* deals with changes in the "inner value of money" (*innere objektive Tauschwert*), which, as Hayek noted, is a somewhat confusing way of dealing with the neutrality of money. The terminology was bound to engender confusion among English readers. The "building block" quality of German undoubtedly makes clear the distinction Mises intended, for those *fluent* in German.

Mises's theory is literally buried in a conventional treatment of monetary inflation. The forced-savings theory follows a cycle theory based on changes in the value of money, in which certain contractual costs are "rigid" in the fact of rising prices. What appeared as an appendage at the time was a radically new theory of cyclical fluctuations.[57]

Mises himself commented obliquely on the disjointedness of his presentation in the Preface to the second German edition:

> I have come to the conclusion that the theory which I put forward as an elaboration and continuation of the doctrines of the Currency School is in itself a sufficient explanation of crisis and not merely a supplement to an explanation in terms of the theory of direct exchange, as I supposed in the first edition.[58]

Hayek referred to Mises's theory as the Wicksell–Mises's theory and stated that progress in monetary theory would depend "partly upon the foundations laid by Wicksell and partly upon criticism of his doctrine." [59]

Hayek broke completely with the quantity-theory approach. The defect in the quantity theory lay in its comparative static approach, lack of attention to adjustment problems, and consequent focus on movements in the price level to the detriment of any analysis of real disturbances. Hayek's criticism thus paralleled Wicksell's.[60] Instead of viewing the proportionality theorem as essential to the quantity theory, he characterized the whole approach of the quantity theorists as "a positive hindrance to further progress." [61] "Hardly any idea in contemporary monetary theory" was not known to writers in the early nineteenth century.[62] In forsaking the approach of microeconomics—"the 'individualistic' method" to which "we owe whatever understanding of economic phenomena we possess"—the quantity theorists were led astray.[63] The quantity-theory approach tended to lead to "three very erroneous opinions":

> *Firstly*, that money acts upon prices and production only if the general price level changes, and, therefore, that prices and production are always unaffected by money,—that they are at their "natural" level,—if the price level remains stable. *Secondly*, that a rising price level tends always to cause an increase of production, and a falling price level always a decrease of production; and *thirdly*, that "monetary theory might even be described as nothing more than the theory of how the value of money is determined." [64]

Here Hayek attacked the very idea to which J. S. Mill had subscribed: that changes in the quantity of money (or the velocity of its circulation) affect only general prices and not relative prices.[65] Hayek saw the proposition that monetary disturbances affect real activity through price level changes to be the logical extension of Mill's analysis. The next step would be to view the business cycle as largely a movement in price levels, with real economic activity being affected only insofar as adjustment to a changing price level is costly.[66]

One must be careful not to read more into the criticism than was there. Hayek regarded the quantity theory as unassailable as a comparative static proposition:

I do not propose to quarrel with the positive content of this theory: I am even ready to concede that so far as it goes it is true, and that, from a practical point of view, it would be one of the worst things which would befall us if the general public should ever again cease to believe in the elementary propositions of the quantity theory.[67]

But like Wicksell, Thornton,[68] Malthus,[69] and many others before him, Hayek believed the quantity theory overlooked *essential* details. The quantity theory had "usurped the central place in monetary theory. . . . Not the least harmful effect of this particular theory is the present isolation of the theory of money from the main body of general economic theory." [70]

Hayek deplored the lack of attention paid by quantity theorists to relative price changes. The title *Prices and Production* was surely chosen to emphasize this argument. Relative prices are what guide production, but, in the divorce of monetary theory from value theory, money is assumed to have no effect on relative prices. Thus by hypothesis money is viewed as having no influence on production. Such was the blind alley into which, Hayek argued, the quantity theory had led economists. Vestiges of the long-run, comparative static approach of classical value theory remained embedded in the quantity theory. It was to this barter model that ignored financial markets that Hayek objected.

The introduction of money does not interfere with the operation of any of the Laws of Value. . . . The relation of commodities to one another remains unaltered by money: the only new relation introduced is their relation to money itself; how much or how little money they will exchange for; in other words, how the Exchange Value of Money itself is determined.[71]

Keynes also reacted against the division between monetary theory and value theory:

So long as economists are concerned with what is called the Theory of Value, they have been accustomed to teach that prices are governed by the conditions of supply and demand; and, in particular, changes in marginal cost and the elasticity of short–period supply have played a prominent part. But when they pass in volume II, or more often in a separate treatise, to the Theory of Money and Prices, we hear no more of these homely but intelligible concepts and move into a world where prices are governed by the quantity of money, by its income–velocity, by the velocity of circulation relatively to the volume of transactions, by hoarding, by forced saving, by inflation and deflation *et hoc genus omne*, and little or no attempt is made to relate these vaguer phrases to our former notions of the elasticities of supply and demand.[72]

Indeed, Hayek had applauded Keynes's first faltering departure from the quantity–theory approach:

That the new approach, which Mr. Keynes has adopted, which makes the rate of interest and its relation to saving and investment the central problem of monetary theory, is an enormous advance on this earlier position [the Cambridge cash–balance theory], and that it directs the attention to what is really essential, seems to me to be beyond doubt.[73]

Again, Hayek's objection to the quantity–theory approach was not a criticism of its positive content, but was, to paraphrase Keynes, an objection to the failure to cast works in this tradition in terms of ordinary economic categories. The quantity theory was an "obstacle" for two reasons: First, from a theoretical view-point, couching a monetary theory of the business cycle in terms of changes in the price level would prejudice readers against other monetary explanations.[74] Thus, the explanation of cyclical fluctuations in terms of changes in the price level was a "naive quantity–theory" explanation,[75] and economists of the stature of Spiethoff rejected all monetary explanations because they identified them with the "naive" quantity theory.[76] Second, the quantity approach led its adherents to erroneously conclude that stabilizing the price level would automatically stabilize economic activity.[77] But, as will be seen, *the major policy conclusion of the Austrian theory of the business cycle is that stabilizing the price level will not, in general, stabilize economic activity.*

Hayek saw Wicksell's and Mises's approach as one that permitted the integration of monetary and value theory. The effect of money on pricing could be taken into account; moreover, money could be shown to have (short-run) effects because changes in the demand for or supply of money alter interest rates, intertemporal prices, and hence the allocation of resources. In current terminology, Hayek's was a theory in which "money mattered."

Hayek systematically criticized theories of cyclical fluctuations in which relative prices—particularly intertemporal prices—played no causal role. While at first he regarded the quantity theory as the chief impediment to progress, he subsequently shifted his attack to the Keynesian economics, or the income-expenditure approach. In Hayek's analysis, both the "naive quantity theory" and Keynesian macroeconomics are cut from the same cloth—the barter conception embodied in Mill's *Principles*. Both analyze economic disequilibrium with the tools of comparative static analysis. And both theories are inherently "macro"—they abstract from changes in relative prices.

To Hayek, Keynes erred in attempting to establish macroeconomic relationships without regard to "the microeconomic structure." [78] "The artificial simplification necessary for macrotheory . . . tends to conceal nearly all that really matters." [79] Keynes's Marshallian and quantity-theory backgrounds lived on in the work that Keynes thought was a "clean break."

NEUTRAL MONEY

Because of Hayek's acceptance of the long-run connection between money and prices, he constructed his business cycle theory as he did. Given his insistence that increases in the money supply (initially) alter relative prices, he was encouraged to seek a mechanism that would restore the original set of relative prices once altered.[80] The theorems of equilibrium states are tools to aid the monetary theorist in analyzing market *tendencies*. Analysis of market adjustment processes indicates when those tendencies may be realized and when thwarted.[81]

Hayek initiated one of the great debates in monetary theory— the debate on the neutrality of money. Today, the concept of the neutrality of money is a bulwark of monetary theory. But the concept is taken to be about long-run effects. However, Hayek, like Keynes, Robertson, and others, wished to analyze the effects of monetary disturbances on economic activity *before equilibrium is restored*. Hayek, like Wicksell was concerned with "what occurs, *in the first place*, with the middle link in the final exchange of one good against another, which is formed by the demand of money for goods and the supply of goods against money." [82]

Keynes might contend that *"the importance of money essentially flows from its being a link between the present and the future."* [83] Myrdal might complain that "most theorists have their early gymnastics in stationary theory and have transferred loose habits of thought to their monetary analysis." [84] And Shackle could describe money as "the refuge from specialized commitment, the postponer of the need to take far-reaching decisions." [85] But all echoed Wicksell in his insistence that monetary analysis is concerned mainly with short-run adjustment; all were concerned with the economics of disequilibrium.

Over the years, English economists, especially at Cambridge, demonstrated little sympathy with Wicksellian or Austrian analysis. Hayek's concept of the "neutrality of money" was also received with some hostility. Sraffa declared:

If Dr. Hayek had adhered to his original intention, he would have seen at once that the differences between a monetary and a non–monetary economy can only be found in those characteristics which are set forth at the beginning of every text–book on money.[86]

To which Hayek responded: "I am, however, not quite sure whether Mr. Sraffa has perceived that the refutation of this idea is one of the central theses of my book." [87]

Nevertheless, the concept of neutral money quickly attracted interest, undoubtedly because of possible applications to monetary policy for mitigating cyclical fluctuations. After the publication of *The General Theory*, interest in the neutrality of money waned.[88] Since Patinkin, economists have employed the concept to show that under stated conditions changes in the quantity of money do not, in the long run, affect either relative prices or real output.[89]

And yet, Hayek employed the very same concept to demonstrate how changes in the quantity of money ordinarily affect interest rates, relative prices, and real economic activity. Indeed, Hayek attracted attention because he demonstrated how monetary disturbances could be nonneutral in their effects.

Hayek's analysis differs from that of contemporary monetary theorists because he focused attention on the short-run effects usually excluded, by assumption, from current theories. He maintained that monetary policy ordinarily has distributional effects that alter relative prices in a predictable way. In fact, an increased quantity of money will cause *ex ante* investment to be larger than *ex ante* saving. *Ex post* saving will equal *ex ante* investment. The difference between *ex ante* and *ex post* saving he termed "forced saving," which leads to an excess accumulation of capital that cannot be maintained.[90]

Hayek's theory of economic fluctuations depends on the soundness of his argument about the nonneutrality of monetary policy; and his treatment of monetary disturbances is intelligible only in terms of his views on forced saving.

FORCED SAVING

Hayek, as an expert on the history of the concept of forced savings, noted that it was first offered in criticism of early quantity-theory analysis. Thus, in commenting on Ricardo's analysis, Malthus stated:

Whenever, in the actual state of things, a fresh issue of notes comes into the hands of those who mean to employ them in the prosecution and extension of profitable business, a difference in the distribution of the circulating medium takes place, similar in kind to that which has been last supposed; and produces similar, though of course comparatively inconsiderable effects, in altering the proportion between capital and revenue in favour of the former. The new notes go into the market as so much additional capital, to purchase what is necessary for the conduct of the concern. But, before the produce of the country has been increased, it is impossible for one person to have more of it, without diminishing the shares of some others. This diminution is affected by the rise of prices, occasioned by the competition of the new notes, which puts it out of the power of those who are only buyers, and not sellers, to purchase as much of the annual produce as before: While all the industrious classes,—all those who sell as well as buy,—are, during the progressive rise of prices, making unusual profits; and even when this progression stops, are left with the command of a greater portion of the annual produce than they possessed previous to the new issues.[91]

Malthus's analysis contained insights that anticipated theoretical developments by Mises, Wicksell, Hayek, and others. An increased quantity of money represents an increased command over real resources. The new money units represent "so much additional capital" to entrepreneurs ("those who mean to employ them in the prosecution and extension of profitable business"). But at full employment, there is a resource constraint, and increased expenditures on capital goods must come at the expense of consumption. Consumers ("those who are only buyers") cannot purchase as many consumer goods as they could before. The mechanism is "the competition of the new notes," which leads to a rise in prices.

Lord Lauderdale spoke of "bank increases [of] the circulating medium of a country" leading to the creation of "a mass of fictitious capital." Dugald Stewart, agreeing with Lord Lauderdale, argued that "the radical evil, in short, seems to be, not the mere over–issue of notes, considered as an addition to our currency, but the anomalous and unchecked extension of *credit* and its inevitable effect in producing a sudden augmentation of prices by a sudden augmentation of demand." [92]

A single concept dominates virtually all discussions of forced saving. Entrepreneurs have an increased command over the scarce resources as the result of an increase in the quantity of money, which enters the system as an increase in credit. The prices of capital goods are bid up, and the production of capital goods is stimulated. Factor incomes are bid up; eventually, the demand for consumption goods increases. But only by this process and in this sequence, do changes in the quantity of money affect prices. That these changes *eventually* affect all prices was not in dispute; the issue was the mechanism by which money affects prices.

Forced saving obviously refers to an *ex post* situation. Consumers find that they must consume less than they had planned at each level of income.[93] Consumer goods are not being produced at the rate at which consumers intend to consume them.[94]

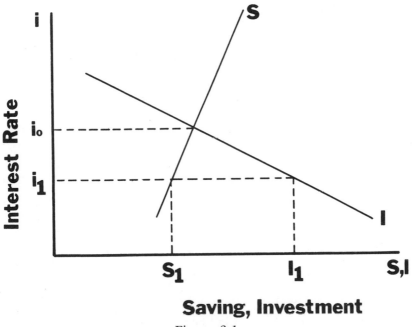

Figure 3.1

The schedules in figure 3.1 refer to planned magnitudes. *Ex post*, investment $(I) = I_1$ and saving (S) is equal in value to investment, I_1. Thus the forced saving is equal to the discrepancy between actual and planned saving $(I_1 - S_1)$.[95] Forced saving occurs during *each period* (in which the quantity of money increases) because of the nonneutral effects of the monetary disturbance. The assumption is that monetary expansion is primarily an increase in the amount of credit available to business.[96] As a consequence, the demand and supply functions that would exist in a barter situation are altered. As Hayek noted in an early work:

The difference between the course of events described by static theory (which only permits movements toward an equilibrium, and which is deduced by directly contrasting the supply of and demand for goods) and the actual course of events [is explained] by the fact that, with the introduction of money (or strictly speaking with the introduction of indirect exchange), a new determining cause is introduced. Money . . . does away with the rigid interdependence and self–sufficiency of the "closed" system of equilibrium, and makes possible movements which would be excluded from the latter.[97]

The concept of the neutrality of money (and thus, indirectly, the concept of forced saving) has frequently been criticized. Piero Sraffa's review of *Prices and Production* was hostile, as I have noted. Others, such as Koopmans and Classen grappled with the theoretical problems raised by the analysis.[98] Again, in the work of recent years dominated by *The General Theory*, that part of the Wicksellian tradition concerned with *relative* prices and so-called distributional effects of monetary policy has been virtually ignored. Of the efforts to save the concept of neutrality of money, Patinkin's is perhaps the most valiant among contemporary writers. But he was hoisted on his own petard. In any comparison between a barter and a money economy, the excess demand functions will *necessarily* differ. Patinkin considered a barter economy as the limiting case of a money economy, that is, one in which the money supply is progressively reduced to zero.

As the nominal quantity of money approaches zero, so does the price level—and at the same rate. Hence the real quantity of money remains unaffected. Thus the limiting position that we have defined as a barter economy is one in which there exists the same *real* quantity of money as in a money economy.[99]

Originally *neutrality* was defined in terms of a congruence between the demand and the supply functions in a barter and a money economy. This comparison is obviously untenable: there is at least one commodity in a money world that is absent from a barter world.[100]

Friedrich Lutz correctly concluded that an important issue was raised by the early neutrality theorists, an issue that becomes obvious in analyzing the conditions under which a *change* in the supply of or demand for money will affect *relative* prices and quantities of nonmoney goods.[101]

As Lutz noted, key differences exist between the work of Wicksell and Hayek, and that of modern monetary economists. Today, neutrality of money follows from standard assumptions of macro models. For Hayek, neutrality of money was a policy goal in a world in which these assumptions did not and could not apply. An important difference exists between monetary theorists concerned with perfecting models (often merely exercises in logic) and earlier monetary theorists trying to explain the world as they perceived it.

The logic of the argument of these more recent writers is unassailable. They have from the start excluded any possible effect of the reduced money rate of interest on the production process by their assumption of the "absence of distribution effects." This assumption allows them to disregard the phenomenon of "forced saving" (which presupposes a shift in income distribution in favour of entrepreneurs or of profit-receivers), and hence to disregard also the related increase in real capital formation. It means that the problem to which earlier writers had attached paramount importance is simply dropped out of the picture. Once we assume that there *are* "distribution effects," the question of what is the right monetary policy if it is desired to aim at the "neutrality" of money inevitably re-emerges.[102]

This reemerging question is the subject of subsequent chapters.

KEYNES ON FORCED SAVING

Keynes's occasional references to Hayek and the Austrians may seem curious, if not quaint—anachronistic discussions of work with no contemporary significance: grist for the mills of historians of thought.[103]

According to Keynes, " 'Forced saving' has no meaning until we have specified some standard rate of saving." The reasonable thing to do would be to select "the rate of saving which corresponds to an established state of full employment. . . . 'Forced saving is the excess of actual saving over what would be saved if there were full employment in a position of long–period equilibrium'." [104] Keynes noted that to Hayek this definition was, in fact, the original meaning of the term.[105]

As Keynes pointed out, the analysis of forced saving needed "some explanation or qualification" to extend it to conditions of less than full employment. However, Keynes accused these theorists *both* of failing to extend the analysis to conditions of less than full employment *and* of doing so without regard to the needed qualifications.[106] Keynes seemed unable to distinguish between the methodological assumption of full employment and the assumption that in fact resources are always fully employed. This is an elementary distinction, concerning which Keynes was neither the first nor the last to be confused.

Obviously, forced saving occurs only in disequilibrium. Hayek used the concept to analyze the impact of a monetary disturbance.[107] Forced saving is empirically important when the quantity of money is increased continually over a prolonged period of time, and the increases occur in the form of increases in the quantity of credit. Hayek investigated this kind of disturbance in *Prices and Production*, and it is to this analysis that we must now turn our attention.

NOTES

1. Harry Johnson, "Monetary Theory and Policy," in *Monetary Theory and Policy*, ed. Richard S. Thorn (New York: Random House, 1969), p. 5 (hereafter, "Monetary Theory").

2. Ibid., p. 5.

3. A strange agglomeration of questions, ancillary to general equilibrium theory, are taken up in monetary theory. Although the term–structure of interest rates is one of these, the determination of "the" interest rate is not. This division has proved less than salutory at times, see Leijonhufvud, *On Keynesian Economics and the Economics of Keynes* (New York: Oxford University Press, 1968), pp. 294-95.

4. For a lively discussion of these controversies, see Johnson, "Monetary Theory," pp. 7-13. After the Johnson survey (1962), a great deal of interest developed in the argument developed by Boris P. Pcsck and Thomas R. Saving in *Money, Wealth, and Economic Theory*, which may be viewed as a continuation of the Patinkin debate (New York: The Macmillan Co., 1967 [hereafter, *Money*]).

5. Milton Friedman, "The Quantity Theory of Money—A Restatement," in *Studies in the Quantity Theory of Money*, ed. idem (Chicago: University of Chicago Press, 1956), pp. 3-21 (hereafter, "Quantity Theory"). On the importance of this paper, see Johnson, "Monetary Theory," pp. 18-19.

6. It is of course largely because of Friedman that there was a revival of interest in the field, however narrowly defined.

7. Friedman, "Quantity Theory," p. 4.

8. Ibid., p. 15.

9. Ibid., p. 15.

10. Milton Friedman, "A Theoretical Framework for Monetary Analysis," *Journal of Political Economy* 78 (March/April 1970): 193-238 (hereafter, "Theoretical Framework"); and idem, "A Monetary Theory of Nominal Income," *Journal of Political Economy* 79 (March/April 1971): 323-37.

11. "For monetary theory, the key question is the process of adjustment to a discrepancy between the nominal quantity of money demanded and the nominal quantity supplied" (Friedman, "Theoretical Framework," p. 225).

The assumption that monetary theory is coextensive with the quantity theory is implicit, for the adjustment to an excess demand for money is the crux of the *quantity theory*.

12. Tobin juxtaposed "monetarists and neo–Keynesians" in a critique of Friedman. Tobin characterized himself as an "eclectic non–monetarist." Non–monetarists appear reluctant to call themselves simply "monetary theorists." "Keynesian" became almost synonymous with *non–monetary* explanation of cyclical fluctuations. Tobin characterized himself as "neo–Keynesian" or "Hicksian," apparently because he believes "that *both* monetary and fiscal policies affect nominal income." He pleaded: "One thing the non–monetarists should *not* be called is '*fiscalists*' " (James Tobin, "Friedman's Theoretical

Framework," *Journal of Political Economy* 80 (September/October 1972):
p. 852).

13. "*Monetary theory* turns out to be simply value theory applied to a
good that has the special technical characteristic of yielding real income
the level of which is directly proportional to the price per unit" (Pesek
and Saving, *Money*, pp. 135-36).

14. Hicks, *Critical Essays in Monetary Theory* (New York: Oxford
University Press, The Clarendon Press, 1967), pp. 61-82.

15. Knut Wicksell, *Lectures on Political Economy*, ed. Lionel Robbins,
2 vols. (London: George Routledge & Sons, 1935), 2:141 (hereafter,
Lectures).

16. Ibid., pp. 143-44.

17. "Consequently, the amount of goods and of transactions being
the same, the value of money is inversely as its quantity multiplied by
what is called the rapidity of circulation" (John Stuart Mill, *Principles of
Political Economy*, ed. William Ashley [Clifton, N. J.: Augustus M. Kelley, 1973], pp. 494, 495). This is J. S. Mill's statement of the proportionality theorem, "other things being the same." Mill then went on to
analyze what occurs when these "other things" are not the same.

18. Schumpeter actually said that "velocity of circulation is an
institutional datum that varies slowly or not at all, but in any case is
independent of prices and volume of transactions." The term *institutional datum* is potentially misleading and associates the theory too
much with the version propounded by one man, Irving Fisher.

19. Joseph A. Schumpeter, *History of Economic Analysis* (New York:
Oxford University Press, 1954), p. 703.

20. David Hume, who in other respects is treated as a major figure
by Schumpeter, surely belongs on the list. Hume argued that "the
prices of commodities are always proportioned to the plenty of money,
and a crown in Harry VII's time served the same purpose as a pound
does at present" (David Hume, "On Money," in *David Hume: Writings on
Economics*, ed. Eugene Rotwein [Madison: University of Wisconsin
Press, 1970], p. 33). Hume's version might be considered the *locus
classicus* (in English) for the quantity theory, as defined above. But the
modernity of Hume's essay is also striking; we still apparently labor
under his first formulation of the effects of money on prices and
output. An incipient monetarism might be inferred in his prescription
against increasing the paper credit of a nation "beyond its natural
proportion to labour and commodities" (Hume, p. 36).

21. Mill, *Principles*, pp. 490-93.

22. Ibid., p. 491.

23. Ibid., p. 492. Mill continued: "If the whole money in circulation
was doubled, prices would be doubled. If it was only increased one–
fourth, prices would rise one–fourth. There would be one fourth more

money, all of which would be used to purchase goods of some description."

24. Ibid., p. 495.

25. Ibid., p. 498.

26. Ibid., pp. 523-41. According to Sowell, "The idea that the price level is *rigidly* linked to the quantity of money by a velocity of circulation which remains constant through all transitional adjustment processes cannot be found in any classical, neoclassical or modern proponent of the quantity theory of money" (Thomas Sowell, *Classical Economics Reconsidered* [Princeton: Princeton University Press, 1974], pp. 59-60).

27. Schumpeter pointed out that after Mill considered the effects of credit, "there is hardly any difference left between Mill's version of the quantity theory and the views of its opponents, contemporaneous or later" (Schumpeter, *History*, p. 705). The reason is that Mill did not subscribe to the quantity theory as defined by Schumpeter.

28. Ricardo's position is clearly stated in *The High Price of Bullion*, reprinted in Piero Sraffa, ed., *Works of David Ricardo*, vol. 3 (Cambridge: Cambridge University Press, 1951) along with a chronology of Ricardo's contributions on this question. Schumpeter remarked that "Ricardo . . . introduced qualifications occasionally and that, here and there, he made statements that were logically incompatible with his strict quantity theory, exactly as he did in the matters of his labour–quantity law of value. In both cases, however, he mentioned them only in order to minimize their importance. . . . We are . . . justified in attributing to him the strict quantity theory, as an approximation" (*History*, pp. 703-4).

29. Adam Smith, *The Wealth of Nations*, ed. Edwin Cannan (New York: Modern Library, 1965), p. 58.

30. According to Smith, laborers could hope to raise their wages above "the lowest which is consistent with common humanity" if the "scarcity of hands occasions a competition among masters, who bid against one another, in order to get workmen." Smith was explicit about the reason for such increased competition: "The demand for those who live by wages, therefore, necessarily increases with the increase of the revenue and stock of every country, *and cannot possibly increase without it* . . . . It is not the actual greatness of national wealth, but its continual increase, which occasions a rise in the wages of labour" (Smith, *Wealth of Nations*, pp. 68-69 [emphasis added]).

31. Sowell, *Classical Economics Reconsidered*, pp. 33-34; see also Frank W. Fetter, "The Relation of Economic Thought to Economic History," *American Economic Review* 55 (May 1965) :138-39.

32. "Ricardian comparative statics and concentration on long run equilibrium assumed away many transitional monetary phenomena, especially in Ricardo's *Principles*—though his polemical pamphlets and correspondence dealt with such problems, even if sometimes some-

what grudgingly" (Sowell, *Classical Economics Reconsidered*, p. 53). For a cost–of–production theorist, the *ultimate* effects of a change in the demand for a commodity money can only be analyzed by taking into account the effects on the cost of production (Mill, *Principles*, pp. 499-506.) But this was too long a run even for Mill and Ricardo. Both analyzed money in terms of demand and supply. Senior remained consistent, however, and insisted on analysis in terms of the cost of production of the metal (Schumpeter, *History*, p. 702).

33. The proportionality theorem does *not* follow from demand-and-supply analysis without further explanation (Schumpeter, *History*, p. 703; Wicksell, *Lectures*, 2: 141-44). On the nature of Ricardo's question, see Wicksell, *Lectures*, 2: 175-76.

34. Henry Thornton, *An Inquiry into the Nature and Effects of the Paper Credit of Great Britain*, ed. F. A. Hayek (London: George Allen & Unwin, 1939), p. 241 (hereafter, *Paper Credit*).

35. Richard Cantillon, quoted in Hayek, *Prices and Production*, 2d ed. (London: Routledge & Kegan Paul, 1935), p. 1.

36. J. S. Mill was concerned with analyzing the effects of monetary disturbances on the purchasing power of money and not on relative prices (*Principles*, pp. 491-93). He treated credit as a substitute for money with similar effects. These effects alter the demand for "goods" (ibid., p. 514). See the text below on forced saving.

37. Ibid., p. 492.

38. Thornton, *Paper Credit*, p. 253.

39. See pp. 40-41 above.

40. J. S. Mill should probably be called a "modified Ricardian" in that he paid more attention to the mechanism by which monetary disturbances are transmitted to real activity than did Ricardo (Mill, *Principles*, pp. 532-41).

41. Schumpeter, *History*, p. 704n. According to Sowell, "Thornton's careful separation of short-run transitional effects from long-run equilibrium contrasts sharply with Ricardo's repeated interpretation of *others'* doctrines in his own comparative statics terms" (*Classical Economics Reconsidered,* p. 58).

42. See p. 38 of text.

43. J. S. Mill recognized the possible distribution effects of an increase in the quantity of money. But he dismissed them as unimportant in the long run. If there were distribution effects, "then until production had accommodated itself to this change in the comparative demand for different things, there would be a real alteration in values . . . . These effects, however, would evidently proceed, not from the mere increase of money, but from accessory circumstances attending it. We are now only called upon to consider what would be the effect of an increase of money considered by itself." That is, he considered the long run effects (Mill, *Principles*, p. 492).

44. See note 31 above.

45. On the tendency of classical economists to recognize but underestimate the short-run effects of a monetary disturbance, see Sowell, *Classical Economics Reconsidered*, pp. 52-66.

46. See note 32 above.

47. Friedman's theoretical framework consists of an analysis of the adjustment to a monetary disturbance and not of propositions about the long-run neutrality of money. "I believe the writings of earlier quantity theorists, from Ricardo and Thornton to Keynes, were not about [the long-run neutrality of money] either" (Milton Friedman, "Comments on the Critics," *Journal of Political Economy* 80 [September/October 1972]: 945). I agree with Friedman on Henry Thornton, just as I disagree with him on Ricardo. Thornton and Ricardo were engaged in entirely different endeavors.

48. According to Anthony Lee, department of economics, University of California at Santa Barbara, no reference to Henry Thornton can be found in any of Wicksell's works (personal communication). If so, this would confirm my hypothesis that Wicksell was not acquainted with the work of the elder Thornton. Most historians of economic thought seem to agree.

49. Ricardo, *Works*, vol. III, p. 91; Robbins, in Wicksell's *Lectures*, 1: xvi-xvii.

50. Axel Leijonhufvud has suggested that Wicksell never had access to a superior library.

51. Wicksell, *Lectures*, 2: 190.

52. The marginal product of investment is Wicksell's marginal productivity of capital, or Jevons's marginal yield of capital (Wicksell, *Lectures*, 1: 147-57; Ralph G. Hawtrey, *Capital and Employment*, 2d ed. [London: Longmans, Green & Co., 1952], p. 29; and Hayek, *Pure Theory of Capital*, p. 189). The term *marginal product* with reference to capital is a misnomer; what is usually meant is the rate of increase in output attributable to an increment to capital.

53. Wicksell, *Lectures*, 2: 192-93. According to Myrdal, Wicksell incorrectly stated the condition of monetary equilibrium as a result (Myrdal, *Monetary Equilibrium*, pp. 126-31).

54. Mises's neglect by American economists is even more egregious than Hayek's. Thus, Mises never benefited from his idea of assisting German refugee intellectuals in finding positions, and he never held a regular academic position in the United States, doubtless because of political discrimination. Mises's place in economics is such that it deserves consideration in a separate work. On Mises's role in Beveridge's plan to help European refugee intellectuals, see Robbins, *Autobiography of an Economist* (London: Macmillan & Co., 1971), pp. 143-44.

55. Keynes is partly responsible for this neglect in Great Britain. Keynes admitted he understood in German what he already knew, yet

he wrote an essentially negative review of Mises's monetary classic, though he later endorsed Mises's basic approach. As Hayek remarked, "He had reviewed L. von Mises' *Theory of Money* for the *Economic Journal* (just as A. C. Pigou had a little earlier reviewed Wicksell) without in any way profiting from it" (Hayek, "Personal Recollections of Keynes and the 'Keynesian Revolution,'" in *A Tiger by the Tail*, ed. Shenoy, p. 101). Keynes reviewed the Mises work in *Economic Journal* 24 (September 1914).

56. Lionel Robbins's Introduction to the *Theory of Money and Credit* (Irvington–on–Hudson, N. Y.: Foundation for Economic Education, 1971). This edition is a reprint of the revised English edition (1952); the first English edition (1934) was based on the second German edition (1924).

57. Mises, *Theory of Money and Credit*, pp. 339-66. The truly Misesian contribution commences on p. 349. If *Prices and Production*, a series of four lectures running over one hundred pages, was overly concise, pity the poor reader confronted with this theory explained in fewer than twenty (albeit lengthier) pages! On the "inner value of money," see Friedrich A. Hayek, *Monetary Theory and the Trade Cycle*, trans. N. Kaldor and H. M. Croome (1933; reprint ed. New York: Augustus M. Kelley, 1966), p. 117 (hereafter, *Monetary Theory*); see also translator's note in *Theory of Money and Credit*, p. 124.

58. Mises, *Theory of Money and Credit*, p. 24.

59. Hayek, *Monetary Theory and the Trade Cycle*, p. 47; and *Prices and Production*, 2d ed. (London: Routledge & Kegan Paul, 1935), p. 26.

60. The period referred to antedated *The General Theory*, and Keynes's own criticism of the quantity-theory tradition.

61. Hayek, *Prices and Production*, p. 4.

62. Ibid., p. 2.

63. Ibid., p. 4.

64. Ibid., p. 7. By "prices" Hayek means relative prices. Footnote reference to Hawtrey omitted.

65. See p. 42 above.

66. Irving Fisher "The Business Cycle Largely a 'Dance of the Dollar,'" *Quarterly Publication of the American Statistical Association*, December, 1923; cited in Hayek, *Monetary Theory and the Trade Cycle*, p. 236n.

67. Hayek, *Prices and Production*, p. 3. The "elementary propositions" would be the *ceteris paribus*, long-run connection between money and prices.

68. See p. 42 above.

69. See footnote 91 for the reference to Malthus's review of Ricardo's *High Price of Bullion*.

70. Hayek, *Prices and Production*, p. 4.

71. J. S. Mill, *Principles*, p. 488. "In considering Value, we were only

concerned with causes which acted upon particular commodities apart from the rest. Causes which affect all commodities alike do not act upon values. But in considering the relation between goods and money, it is with causes that operate upon all goods whatever that we are specially concerned. We are comparing goods of all sorts on one side, with money on the other side, as things to be exchanged against each other" (ibid., p. 491).

72. Keynes, *General Theory*, p. 292.

73. Hayek, "Reflections on the Pure Theory of Money of Mr. J. M. Keynes," part 1, *Economica* 11 (August 1931): 270. Hayek was here reviewing *The Treatise*.

74. See the text below pp. 95-96, for a discussion of whether Hayek's was a monetary explanation.

75. Hayek, *Monetary Theory*, p. 105.

76. Ibid., pp. 104-6; this work was written for a German audience.

77. See Hayek, *Prices and Production*, pp. 28-29.

78. Hayek, "Personal Recollections of Keynes and the 'Keynesian Revolution,'" p. 102.

79. Ibid., p. 106.

80. Friedrich A. Hayek, "Three Elucidations of the Ricardo Effect," *Journal of Political Economy* 77 (March/April 1969): 279-81.

81. See Hayek, "Economics and Knowledge," in *Individualism and Economic Order* (Chicago: University of Chicago Press, 1948), p. 45.

82. Wicksell, *Lectures*, 2: 159 (emphasis in original).

83. Keynes, *General Theory*, p. 293 (emphasis in original).

84. Myrdal, *Monetary Equilibrium*, p. 45.

85. Shackle, *Years of High Theory* (Cambridge: Cambridge University Press, 1967), p. 6.

86. Piero Sraffa, "Dr. Hayek on Money and Capital," *Economic Journal* 42 (March 1932): 43.

87. Hayek, "Money and Capital: A Reply," *Economic Journal* 42 (June 1932): 238.

88. "[Keynes] was little concerned with relative prices" (Friedrich A. Lutz, "On Neutral Money," in *Roads to Freedom*, eds. Erich Streissler, et al. [New York: Augustus M. Kelley, 1969], p. 112).

89. Ibid., pp. 112-14; Don Patinkin, *Money, Interest, and Prices*, 2d ed. (New York: Harper & Row, 1965), pp. 175-76.

90. The details of his analysis of the changes in real economic activity are considered in chapters 4 and 5 of this study.

91. Cited by Hayek, *Prices and Production*, pp. 19-20.

92. Hayek, "A Note on the Development of the Doctrine of 'Forced Saving'," *Profits, Interest, and Investment* (New York: Augustus M. Kelley, 1970), p. 190.

93. *Which* consumers would be expected to engage in the forced saving will be discussed in chapter 5.

94. Hayek, *Prices and Production*, pp. 87-88. Thus, forced saving is not a sum of money that consumers are forced to save. On this, see W. E. Kuhn, *The Evolution of Economic Thought*, 2d ed. (Cincinnati: South–Western Publishing Co., 1970), p. 386.

95. Strictly speaking, Hayek designated "forced saving" as the difference between consumption before the monetary disturbance and that after, or the difference between equilibrium saving and the higher level of investment, I_1 (Hayek, *Prices and Production*, p. 57.) But in keeping with contemporary analysis, which focuses on planned magnitudes at current prices, I have defined forced saving somewhat differently in the text. The S function represents the supply of *voluntary* (i.e., planned) saving; it is not the standard "supply of loanable funds" curve. A chief purpose of this analysis is to distinguish between loanable funds composed of voluntary savings and those that are not.

96. "The case most frequently to be encountered in practice [is that] of an increase of money in the form of credits granted to producers" (Hayek, *Prices and Production*, p. 54).

97. Hayek, *Monetary Theory*, pp. 44-45.

98. See Lutz, "On Neutral Money," pp. 105-9. The reader may detect a similarity between my analysis of the problem and that of Lutz. While I had considered these issues before reading Lutz and had arrived at a similar—though not identical—position, I was influenced by his analysis.

99. Patinkin, *Money, Interest, and Prices*, p. 75.

100. It is possible to conceive of money in this context as the *numéraire* of Walras's system: "Money in this latter sense is introduced, after the relative prices have been determined, in the shape of a money equation which sets the general price level while leaving relative prices unaffected" (Lutz, "On Neutral Money," p. 107). But this concept of money would do violence to the work of Wicksell, Hayek, and others.

101. Ibid., p. 112.

102. Ibid., p. 116.

103. Keynes, *General Theory*, pp. 39, 59-60, 76, 79-80, 176, 183, 192-93, 214, 328-29.

104. Ibid., p. 80. Keynes continued: "This definition would make good sense, but a sense in which a forced excess of saving would be a very rare and a very unstable phenomenon, and a forced *deficiency* of saving the usual state of affairs" (*General Theory*, p. 80). It is the first two propositions (that is, that forced saving is "rare" and that it is "unstable") that are at issue. The third proposition is one of which I can make no sense, unless Keynes wished to maintain that we suffer chronic unemployment. Such cryptic remarks led Hayek to conclude that Keynes believed that unemployment was chronic and to criticize Keynes's "economics of abundance" (*Pure Theory of Capital*, pp. 373-75).

105. Keynes here referred to Hayek's article "A Note on the De-

velopment of the Doctrine of 'Forced Saving'," reprinted in *Profits, Interest, and Investment*, pp. 183-97.

106. Keynes, *General Theory*, pp. 80-81. See the caveat in note 95 above. Keynes's treatment of forced saving is an instance of how his solecistic use of "classical" led him into error. He argued that "the usual classical assumption [is] that there is always full employment" (*General Theory*, p. 191). What is true is that Ricardians were virtually always concerned with the long run, in which *ex hypothesi* there is full employment. In Keynes's terminology, forced saving theorists were "classical." Hence, the reasoning goes, they thought there was always full employment, etc. Keynes cited no reference on forced saving, except Hayek's note on the history of the concept. It is doubtful whether Keynes could have found any support for his argument.

107. Hayek, "Three Elucidations," pp. 279-80.

4

Money and Prices

By the same act with which a bank increases the circulating medium of a country, it issues into the community a mass of fictitious capital, which serves not only as circulating medium but creates an additional quantity of capital to be employed in every mode in which capital can be employed (Lord Lauderdale, cited in Hayek, *Profits, Interest, and Investment,* p. 190).

THE UNIVERSITY OF LONDON LECTURES

Friedrich A. Hayek was invited to deliver the special university lectures at the London School of Economics during the 1930-31 session. In the space of four lectures, subsequently published under the title *Prices and Production*, he analyzed the microeconomics of the "typical nineteenth century business cycle." [1] What he actually did in less than 150 pages was potentially even more far reaching: he integrated monetary theory and price theory more fully than had been done before.[2] The goal of current work in the integration of macrotheory and microtheory is essentially the same as Hayek's, and I believe progress would have been much greater had the contributions of Hayek not been lost sight of in the aftermath of the Keynesian revolution.

The other major monetary theorists of the day were similarly engaged in a reexamination of business cycle theory. Notable among them were J. M. Keynes, D. H. Robertson, and R. G. Hawtrey in England; Irving Fisher and Henry Simons in the United States; Ludwig von Mises and Gunnar Myrdal on the Continent; and, indeed, virtually the entire membership of the Austrian and Swedish schools. The Continental and British monetary theorists—intellectually Hayek straddled these groups—were more intent than the Americans on finding microfoundations for their theories. These divergent thinkers had a common purpose: to achieve the integration of monetary and price theory.[3] All were profoundly dissatisfied with the state of monetary theory in its many variants.[4]

Hayek's business cycle theory, as presented to his English readers, was a blend of monetary theory, capital theory, and price theory. The lectures were first published in 1931. (His 1928 work on the monetary questions raised by the study of cyclical fluctuations was not translated into English until 1933 and was therefore unavailable to his English audience.)[5] Hayek viewed the price mechanism as a system of signals and the "economic problem" as one of social coordination. However, these conceptions were undeveloped until his contributions to the Socialist-calculation debates and the tetrad on economic coordination, of which "Economics and Knowledge" was the first.[6] These articles for the most part were written after his initial work on cyclical fluctuations was translated into English.

Many of the substantive issues treated by Hayek can be examined without detailed development of Austrian capital theory. At times, Austrian capital theory can be so idiosyncratic that communication with those unfamiliar with it is impeded, as Hayek recognized in later writings.[7] Reference to its characteristic propositions will be made insofar as this aids in the subsequent analysis.

THE INFLATION PROCESS AND RESOURCE ALLOCATION

To Hayek there was one essential fact about the business cycle to be explained by any theory of economic fluctuations:

The task [of understanding the business cycle] is made rather easier by the fact that there does exist to–day, on at least one point, a far-reaching agreement among the different theories. They all regard the emergence of a *disproportionality* among the various productive groups, and in particular the excessive production of capital goods, as the first and main thing to be explained.[8]

Gottfried Haberler, more than a decade later, had a similar view, though he no longer accepted the particulars of the Mises-Hayek account. He stated that there are "two features which can be observed in every cycle, probably without exception, although they are not implied by our definition of the cycle."

They are (1) that cyclical fluctuations in production and employment are "accompanied by a parallel movement of the money value of production and transactions," and (2) "that cyclical fluctuations are more marked in connection with the production of producer's goods than in connection with the production of consumers' goods." [9]

Hayek expanded on the theories of Wicksell and Mises to account for a particular phenomenon—the so-called volatility of investment, or the "disproportionality" in production.[10] A process of inflation, or more precisely "cyclical expansion," was seen to consist of a reallocation of resources from industries producing consumer goods (or "final output") to those producing intermediate products. If a cyclical expansion starts from conditions of actual general resource unemployment, then expansion could, for a time, occur in all industries simultaneously. Hayek did not see the expansion as being uniform in practice, and his theory attempted to account for this nonuniformity. He developed a theory of the transmission mechanism of monetary disturbances, in which a change in the growth rate of the money stock depresses the complex of market interest rates below an equilibrium level.[11] Investment is stimulated, and through the augmentation in money expenditures on capital goods factor incomes are bid up, and finally the prices of consumption output rise. The complex allocation questions involved in this process are analyzed in *Prices and Production*.

Hayek did not treat the "excessive production of capital goods" as the only feature of a business cycle, though he considered it the most important one. Any tendency for the prices of all goods to change was treated as a secondary phenomenon. He did not view changes in price levels as a necessary condition for a business cycle.[12]

Hayek perceived the necessity for explaining the emergence of resource unemployment in any theory of cyclical fluctuations. However, his approach in *Prices and Production* created a good deal of controversy: he started with an assumption of full employment, that is, long-run equilibrium. He did not, however, assume that the economy would remain at full employment. His object was to focus on certain processes that he thought would occur during any actual cyclical upswing as full employment was approached. Indeed, if Hayek's analysis of the impact of changes in the growth rate of the money stock is correct, these processes are inevitable in such expansions.

In considering Hayek's approach, a distinction must be made between the *methodological* assumption of full employment and the *empirical* assumption of full employment. The methodological assumption of full employment has three distinct advantages. First, it is consistent with the general approach in other areas of economic theory. Starting from full employment (i.e., equilibrium) avoids attributing adjustments that would occur in any case to the disturbance under consideration. Next, it focuses attention on the problem to be analyzed—that of unemployment—and compels the theorist to deduce the emergence of unemployed resources rather than beg the question by assuming what needs to be explained.[13] Finally, it minimizes the possibility of constructing a theory—believed to be *general*—that is contingent on the existence of unemployed resources throughout the economy.[14] A number of critics, including a friendly expositor of Hayek's ideas, have failed to note the aforementioned distinction and Hayek's own strictures on the subject.[15]

Hayek was not the first to be attacked for assuming full employment. After Keynes set the example of reconstructing theories out of whole cloth, the classical economists became subject to this charge. While economists of the nineteenth century undoubtedly wrote *as though* there were ordinarily no unemployed resources, I know of no major figure who denied the existence of unemployed resources. Furthermore many attempted to explain the phenomenon, even though it was not their chief policy concern.[16]

Although older generations of economists had virtually no theoretical explanation for large-scale unemployment not due to wage controls or other direct market interventions, contemporary economic theory does little more. The worker–search hypothesis leaves much to be desired. As William H. Hutt noted, Keynesian macrotheory has not produced a theory of unemployment at all; at best it offers a theory of aggregate demand.[17] Seldom has the ancient admonition regarding the throwing of stones in glass houses been more applicable than to critics of classical and allegedly classical treatments of unemployment.

THE PRODUCTION PROCESS

In *Prices and Production* Hayek developed a "goods in process" model, in which land and labor services pass through successive *stages of production* until consumer goods finally emerge. A "stage" consists of some productive activity (for example, stamping out parts with a mold). An entire *process of production* consists of many stages with the goods processed at each stage called *intermediate products*. A change in the number of stages or the reallocation of factors among stages is described as a change in the structure of production.[18] A consumer good yields all its services in a single period; by this definition Hayek circumvented the durable–goods problem.[19] His purpose was to emphasize an aspect of capital to which he felt insufficient attention had been paid.[20] This is the distribution of capital goods in time. In Hayek's metaphorical analysis, intermediate products flow as from tributaries into successive stages of production, and the value of intermediate products at any point in the stream is a function of time, $f(t)$. The total value of the intermediate products is thus the integral of this function over a period r, equal to the length of the adopted process of production. Beginning at time x, the total value of the intermediate products is:

$$\int_{x.}^{x+r} f(t)\ dt$$

According to Hayek, the output of consumer goods (that is, the rate at which consumer goods appear) is a function of this time interval, $f(x+r)$. Thus the Hayek model is expressed purely in terms of flows. The reasons Hayek did not attempt to translate the model into one couched in terms of both stocks and flows are several.

First, there is the inherent difficulty of including durable goods in a model of this type: "The different instalments of future services which such goods are expected to render will . . . have to be imagined to belong to different 'stages' of production corresponding to the time interval which will elapse before these services mature." [21] Hayek also initially assumed that at each stage the intermediate products are exchanged for money; there is no vertical integration. If durable capital goods were included, the individual must be assumed to be renting the capital goods from himself.[22] Finally, and most important, Hayek felt that in ordinary analysis too much attention is accorded to the *durability* of particular capital goods in explaining the effects of changes in the rate of interest on its value.

It is not the individual durability of a particular good but the time that will elapse before the final services to which it contributes will mature that is regarded as the decisive factor. That is, it is not the attributes of the individual good but its position in the whole time structure of production that is regarded as relevant.[23]

The model of *Prices and Production* emphasizes the "time structure of production." Hayek employed "Jevonian Investment Figures" as a pedagogic device to illustrate the production process:

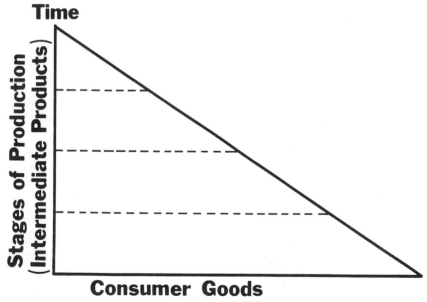

Figure 4.1

In figure 4.1 the horizontal side of the triangle represents the output of consumption goods $f(x+r)$; the hypotenuse, the production function, $f(t)$; and the area, the integral that appears above.[24] The various stages of production—the horizontal segments of the diagram—consist of circulating capital (measured in value terms).

Was Hayek attempting to measure the aggregate capital stock in *Prices and Production*? The answer is in doubt. Although he did not produce such a measure, he created the impression that there is some basis for doing so. Thus, he referred to the "proportion between the amount of intermediate products . . . and the amount of . . . output" increasing as the duration of the production process increases.[25] He also described production as becoming more "capitalistic" as "the average time interval between the application of the original means of production and the completion of the consumers' goods increases." [26] While his use of "capitalistic" is loose, it suggests a capital-output ratio. What he actually measured was the value (in consumption output) to which an input will grow (that is, the compounded value of an investment).

Hayek's lack of precision in *Prices and Production* on this matter is notable on several counts. Even in terms of his own endeavor, he had no need to make use of aggregate concepts; indeed, he disparaged such aggregative procedures. He generally objected to the treatment of capital goods as homogenous. In *The Pure Theory of Capital* he pointed out that in principle it is impossible to measure capital stock by reference to an average period of investment, even if the rate of interest is already given.[27]

I believe Hayek adopted a most "un–Hayekian" procedure in *Prices and Production*. He treated consumer goods as homogeneous if they are available in the same time period. Analysis applicable to the production of a particular consumer good is carried over to the aggregate output of consumer goods. He in effect adopted a one output–good model, though he was quite explicit at other places about the difficulties that arise from the existence of heterogeneous capital goods. Yet having treated consumption output as homogeneous, he also treated capital goods as inchoate consumer goods even though he specifically rejected this view at other times. In every other context Hayek was a trenchant critic of attempts to treat "capital" as a fund or as an amount of waiting.[28]

Hayek was quite open about the deficiencies of *Prices and Production*. He considered himself fortunate to have received an offer to deliver the University of London lectures when he did. When the invitation arrived, he was convinced the central ideas of *Prices and Production* were correct, and he presented them in their simplicity.

In *Prices and Production* Hayek was almost offhand about the necessary conditions for equilibrium, or correspondence between the plans of consumers and producers: "The proportion of money spent for consumers' goods and money spent for intermediate products is equal to the proportion between the total demand for consumers' goods and the total demand for the intermediate product necessary for their continuous production." [29] In a lecture delivered less than three years after the University of London lectures, he was far more precise about the conditions for equilibrium. Describing his theory as "the 'Wicksellian' theory of crises" he remarked that it is "quite independent of any idea of absolute changes in the quantity of capital and therefore of the concepts of saving and investment in their traditional sense." Hayek continued:

The starting point for a fully developed [business cycle] theory . . . would be (a) the intentions of all the consumers with respect to the way in which they wish to distribute at all the relevant dates all their resources (not merely their 'income') between current consumption and provision for future consumption, and (b) the separate and independent decisions of the entrepreneurs with respect to the amounts of consumers' goods which they plan to provide at these various dates. Correspondence between these two groups of decisions would be characteristic of the kind of equilibrium which we now usually describe as a state where savings are equal to investments and with which the idea of an equilibrium rate of interest is connected.[30]

For Hayek, the crucial question for business cycle theory was the mutual correspondence of the plans of savers and investors and those of consumers and producers. Before asking how an economy can be in disequilibrium, he sought to posit the theoret-

ical conditions under which the system would be "in equilibrium." [31]

An essential difference exists between a change in the structure
of production resulting from increased saving and a change
from an increase in the supply of money through bank loans to
producers (at a lower rate of interest than previously was the
case).[32] The alternative methods of financing the same increase
in investment may be illustrated as a first approximation as
follows:

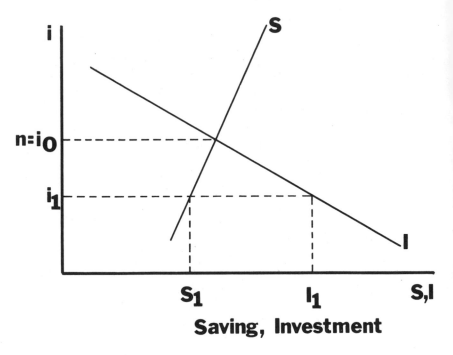

Figure 4.2

If increased investment is the consequence of a change in the
propensity to save, then savings (S) and investment (I) will be
equalized at a market rate of interest, i_0, which will be equal to the
natural, or equilibrium, rate, n. If the increased investment is
financed, not by increased saving, but by an amount of bank
credit being extended per period (equal to the difference be-

tween I_1 and S_1), then the loan rate, i will be below the natural rate, n. This natural rate is the rate of interest at which the flow of consumer and producer goods being produced and sold on the market is the same as the flow of expenditures on such goods. It is the rate at which the *ex ante* decisions of producers and consumers are mutually consistent.[33]

This approach can, however, only be a beginning, for it is quintessentially macro in conception. Consequently, it ignores problems crucial to Hayek's analysis. The saving–investment analysis presented here involved the aggregation of the separate micro–investment functions. Hayek considered this procedure to be suspect in ignoring the shift effects on the separate investment demand curves of changes in the rate of interest (changes which merely move one down this constant aggregate investment function). Also according to Hayek:

Whether we are able to decide what savings and what investment are depends . . . on whether we can give the idea of maintaining capital intact a clear and realistic meaning . . . . As soon, however, as one makes any serious attempt to answer this question, one finds not only that the concept of the maintenance of capital has no definite meaning, but also that there is no reason to assume that even the most rational and intelligent entrepreneur will ever in dynamic conditions be either willing or able to keep his capital constant in any quantitative sense, that is with respect to any of the measurable properties of capital itself.[34]

To recast the saving-investment analysis in *net* terms, the concept of maintaining capital intact must be clarified; yet entrepreneurs do not necessarily keep the *value* of their capital intact. These difficulties with saving-investment analysis must be noted lest serious confusion arise as the result of what is said later.

An increase in the propensity to save, according to Hayek, will not initiate a cyclical expansion.[35] Rather, the phenomenon is useful in explaining the movement of relative prices during a credit expansion (that is, when voluntary saving has *not* changed). Whether an increase in saving is necessarily transmitted into increased investment is not considered. Like Wicksell, Hayek assumed that the financial sector does nothing to impede this process.[36]

With an increase in saving, the impact of the concomitant decrease in consumption demand on producers who put the "final touches" on consumer goods is obvious—they find their receipts falling. However, along with the decreased receipts from current consumption there is an increase in funds available for future consumption output. In the final stages of production (that is, those nearest the production of consumer goods) the decrease in costs will not offset the decrease in receipts. Increased expenditures elsewhere maintain, even augment, factor costs. The price margin between output and input—from whence the return on capital emerges—narrows. Employment of funds in the final stage of production becomes less attractive than its employment at other stages. Funds will tend to be shifted to earlier stages of production at the same time new savings are being made available. The production stage preceding the final stage will also experience a narrowing of price margins, as will the stage prior to that, and so on. But more funds will be available in early stages, and at some point the tendency for a rise in the prices of the products of early stages (that is, those farthest in time from the production of consumption goods) will overcome the tendency for a fall in prices. Indeed, it will pay to begin new stages of production. An intertemporal reallocation of factor services occurs as a consequence of intertemporal changes in relative prices.[37]

A narrowing of price margins leads to a shifting of capital among stages. The *investment period* increases.[38] A switch to the longer investment period occurs because it is not profitable to employ the older and quicker production methods. Investment projects with lower yields relative to prevailing rates of return acquire a positive present value. Economic losses are incurred on some old investments.

Hayek employed a *discounted* value of the marginal product theory of factor remuneration. Increased saving leads to a fall in the rate of interest. As a first approximation, the prices of land and labor services are bid up as the rate of interest falls. In this first approximation, land and particularly labor are treated as homogeneous.

To Hayek, a decrease in the interest rate may be translated into the proposition that both wage rates and land rents have risen relative to the prices of the products they help produce. As the interest rate falls, price margins between stages narrow, for real factor costs are increasing. The fall in prices of the products of the later stages of production is partly responsible for this narrowing of price margins.[39]

Hayek's proposition must be distinguished from one particularly common misinterpretation. Were this a valid conceptual experiment, a fall in the rate of interest would, other things equal, increase the demand-price schedules for *all* assets. But formulating the experiment in *ceteris paribus* terms overlooks the *mutatis mutandis* conditions of the disturbance. The very process that affects the interest rate alters the size of the quasi–rents accruing to the heterogenous capital goods, which are combined according to particular expectations that will be falsified (by the assumed disturbance). This process is not to be relegated to the second order of magnitude, as is usually done.[40] In his criticism of Keynes's *Treatise*, Hayek observed:

Capitalization is not so directly an *effect* of the rate of interest; it would be truer to say that both are effects of one common cause, viz. the scarcity or abundance of means available for investment, relative to the demand for those means. Only by changing this relative scarcity will a change in the Bank Rate also change the demand price for the services of fixed capital.[41]

Although fixed capital was excluded from the model of *Prices and Production*, the essence of the problem remained, that is, to demonstrate the effects of a change in intertemporal consumption demand—or an *apparent* change—and the consequent change in relative factor scarcities on the pattern of investment.

In terms of Hayek's investment diagram, there will be a narrowing of the base and a lengthening of the vertical side. Increased investment will be distributed both as an increase in resources in early stages and an addition of new stages. Only by this process are rates of return on all investments equalized. The investment must take the form of capital "deepening" rather than capital "widening" in the absence of any unemployed land and labor.

Ralph Hawtrey introduced the terms *capital widening* and *capital deepening*:

The process of which the capital equipment of a community is increased may take two forms, a "widening" and a "deepening." The widening of the capital equipment means the extension of productive capacity by the flotation of new enterprises, or the expansion of existing enterprises, without any change in the amount of capital employed for each unit of labour. The deepening means an increase in the amount of capital employed for each unit of labour.[42]

Hawtrey concluded that a reduction in the rate of interest "is a sign that the widening of capital is insufficient to use up the resources of the investment market." [43]

The process of capital deepening will be accompanied by capital widening in particular industries. This fact is implied in the Hayek's schematic analysis in *Prices and Production*—more is invested in early stages and less in late stages. Capital deepening might be defined as capital narrowing in the later stages, concomitant with capital widening in earlier stages.[44]

Pace Hawtrey, capital deepening may be analyzed without reference to aggregate capital measure. One need only say that capital will be invested in different ways and in different goods (and outline in what general direction changes will be made). Hayek particularly did not need to refer to an aggregate capital measure. But as late as 1941 he spoke, as did Hawtrey, of "providing an unchanged number of workmen with more (or more elaborate) equipment." [45] This situation results when the investment period tends to lengthen as a result of the same conditions that bring about a fall in interest rates. As interest rates fall, however, the relative prices of various capital goods change, and new types of capital goods are substituted. The units will be incommensurable, and we cannot be sure what will happen to the value of the capital stock.[46] Indeed, Hayek pointed out that changes in the structure of production may be analyzed without reference to aggregate capital stock or an average period of investment.[47] We need only speak of marginal adjustments in the pattern of investment.

Hayek was more circumspect in *The Pure Theory of Capital* than

in *Prices and Production*. He pointed out that "most of the changes
in productive technique are likely to involve changes in the
investment periods of different units of input to a different
degree and perhaps in different directions." [48] A "change in the
length of the process" could be employed to describe a situation
where changes are "predominantly in one direction." [49] Though
Hayek slipped into less precise and less guarded modes of expression, his final opinion was as follows: "For our present
purposes we do not need to know whether a whole process as
such is longer or shorter than another." [50] Nor apparently do we
need to know anything about the aggregate capital stock or
capital per head.

A critical question for Hayek is whether the effects of an
increase in saving in a money economy are the same as in a barter
situation. Of the effects of an increase in saving in a money
economy, he observed: "The effect thus realized . . . is one which
fulfills the object of saving and investing, and is identical with the
effect which would have been produced if the savings were made
in kind instead of in money." [51] Of course, if the saving were
made in kind, the process would not occur in the same way,
unless we are to assume money does not facilitate exchange! "It is
self–contradictory to discuss a process which admittedly could
not take place without money, and at the same time to assume
that money is absent or has no effect." [52] The justifiable conclusion of *Prices and Production* is that changes from the increase in
saving lead to a new *stable* equilibrium. This is not necessarily the
equilibrium that would obtain in a barter situation, assuming
attaining equilibrium would be possible.[53]

THE EFFECTS OF CREDIT

Hayek always treated the distinction between real and monetary changes as fundamental. Real changes (for example, a
change in tastes, or in time preference) lead to changes in money
expenditures, which in turn bring about equilibrium realloca-
tions. On the other hand, he treated monetary changes (for
example, a change in the money supply) as "self–reversing" and

the temporary equilibria created by such changes as "inherently unstable." [54] This is the principal thesis of *Prices and Production*, where Hayek contrasted the effects of an autonomous increase in the money stock with those of an increase in the rate of saving.[55]

The immediate impact of an increase in the money stock (which by assumption is an increase in bank credit) is the same for transactors as a shift in the savings function. The reason is that both disturbances generate the same signals in the loan market—the interest rates fall.[56] In the case of a shift in the savings function, the resulting changes involve a transition to a new equilibrium of the kind assumed in barter theory. If fluctuations in savings are violent and frequent, cyclical fluctuations may be observed in the absence of additional monetary disturbances. But Hayek contended that "experience provides no ground for assuming that such violent fluctuations in the rate of savings will occur otherwise than in consequence of crises." [57]

The impression from reading *Prices and Production* is that in the absence of credit creation by the banking system, the real economy is fundamentally stable. The actions of transactors in the aggregate are not "perverse." Increases in the propensity to save with resulting changes in the pattern of investment are not suddenly reversed. Transactors do not save in order to lure unsuspecting entrepreneurs into (*ex post*) foolish investments, and then withdraw their savings at the crucial moment, thus to wreak havoc on interdependent investment plans.

Hayek focused on the market signals employed by savers and investors in making their decisions, which, though *independently* arrived at, are *interdependent*. He sought to demonstrate how a general inconsistency of plans could come about. As he phrased it, "We might have to distinguish between what we may call justified errors, caused by the price system, and sheer errors about the course of external events." [58] He had an hypothesis: "It seems . . . more likely that they [entrepreneurs] may all be equally misled by following guides or symptoms which as a rule prove reliable." [59]

The signals followed by market decision makers are relative prices, precisely because this procedure has a demonstrated survival value. However, there are times when they prove undependable, that is, there are periods of economic disequilibria in which relative prices function so as to discoordinate the economic activity of savers and investors. This observation neither supports the contention that decentralized decision making is inherently "irrational" nor explains why the price system can misfunction. For these explanations one must turn to capital and monetary considerations. The problem was aptly phrased by an expositor of Hayek's theories:

Pricing . . . is . . . a continuous information–collecting and disseminating process, but it is the institutional framework that determines both the extent to which, and the degree of success with which, prices are enabled to perform this potential signalling or allocative function.[60]

The assumption of *Prices and Production* is that the capital goods industries or earlier stages of production can expand (that is, switch to more "capitalistic" methods) only at the cost of present consumption. But in the case of a monetary expansion

this sacrifice is not voluntary, and is not made by those who will reap the benefit from the new investments. It is made by the consumers in general who, because of the increased competition from the entrepreneurs who have received the additional money, are forced to forego part of what they used to consume. It comes about not because they want to consume less, but because they get less goods for their money income. There can be no doubt that, if their money receipts should rise again, they would immediately attempt to expand consumption to the usual proportion.[61]

Let us assume for the moment that consumers' command over resources again increases at some point. There is no reason to expect that, once consumers' incomes rise, there will be any change in the desired consumption–saving ratio out of that level of income. But the constancy of saving necessitates a return to the previous, "less capitalistic" method of production. It is this contraction process that Hayek explained most fully in a series of articles on the Ricardo effect, an effect that we will examine in the following chapter.

In terms of the investment diagram, the change to a narrower base and a heightened altitude will be reversed. But with the

increased amount of money in circulation (assuming no endogenous deflation of the money stock as part of the cyclical
decline in economic activity), the dollar value of goods sold in
each stage will be greater. In other words, the standard long-run
comparative static conclusions of the quantity theory are preserved. Indeed, once one admits that money is *not* neutral in the
short run, and that there are relative price effects of sufficient
duration that time-consuming production processes are altered,
one is virtually *compelled* to accept the plausibility of the *self–
reversing* features of a monetary disturbance; that is, one must so
long as one believes that the absolute quantity of money is of no
significance in the *long run*, and that the economy cannot be in
neutral equilibrium for any conceivable set of relative prices.

HICKS ON HAYEK

Forced saving plays a crucial role in Hayek's malinvestment
theory.[62] If saving, *ex post*, is greater than it would be at full
employment, then so is investment. Hayek employed the theory
of forced saving to demonstrate that under some conditions
malinvestment would occur. The conclusion is hardly startling
given the assumption that the rate of interest at which entrepreneurs can borrow is below the equilibrium (natural) rate of
interest.

Yet a number of economists have had difficulty in perceiving
how Hayek arrived at this conclusion. Hicks commented that, if
forced saving takes place, "there has to be a lag of consumption
behind wages." But he concluded that "obviously this lag is not
acceptable." [63] Where did Hicks and Hayek part company?

Hicks continued to work on the problem. But their "parting of
the ways was on the issue of the effects of money on decision
making." Hicks argued subsequently that Hayek's analysis "was
mixed up, in that exciting work, with monetary considerations
that do not really belong." [64] No sense can be made of the arguments in *Prices and Production* if one adopts the view that the
"monetary considerations . . . do not really belong." Indeed, the
monetary considerations probably are the most original con-

tribution of the analysis. One could disagree with the details of the production theory and still accept the monetary theory. *Prices and Production* simply does not "work" without the monetary analysis—at least not as a theory of economic fluctuations. This is what Hicks in fact demonstrated in "The Hayek Story" and why the Hayek story must be retold.

Without the doctrine of forced saving induced by bank credit expansion, there is no logic to the lag of consumption behind income. Hicks tried "sticky wages" (which are not in *Prices and Production*—at least not wages "sticky upwards"), but noted that "if one pursues this line of thought, one is led towards a theory which is more like that of Keynes, or perhaps of Robertson, than of Hayek." [65]

Hicks finally tried to mend *Prices and Production*: "Suppose that one had *not* started with a 'credit expansion' but had begun with . . . a genuine increase in the propensity to save." [66] What follows is a tortured transformation of a theory of short-run disturbances into "a forerunner of the growth theory of more recent years." [67] It is no accident that only in this guise did Hicks contend "we can still make something of it [*Prices and Production*]." [68] For what Hicks outlined is a *barter theory* of growth-induced disturbances. [69]

Forced saving occurs because entrepreneurs are given the means by the banking system to appropriate a larger portion of the economy's scarce resources. It must be emphasized that Hayek never dealt with a single "one shot" increase in the money supply. [70] In his response to Hicks's 1967 work, Hayek emphasized that the continual injection of money was in the form of business loans:

This process can evidently go on indefinitely, at least as long as we neglect changes in the manner in which expectations concerning future prices are formed. Whatever the lag between the impact effect of the new expenditures on a few prices affected immediately and the spreading of this effect to any other prices, the distortion of the "equilibrium" price structures corresponding to the "real" data must continue to exist. The extra demand which continually enters in the form of newly created money remains one of the constant data determining a price structure adjusted to this demand. However short the lag between one price change and the effect of the expenditure of the increased receipts on other prices, and as long as the process of change in the total money stream continues, the changed relationship between particular prices will also be preserved.[71]

Two concepts come together in Hayek's theory: the Thornton–Wicksell analysis of the effects of a divergence between the loan and equilibrium rates of interest, and the doctrine of forced saving. Hicks tried to abstract from monetary considerations in his reconstruction of Hayek's argument:

The "reduction" of the market rate below the natural rate must therefore be interpreted as a disequilibrium phenomenon; a phenomenon that can only persist while the markets are out of equilibrium. As soon as equilibrium is restored, equality between market and natural rate must be restored. Thus there is no room for a prolonged discrepancy between market rate and natural rate if there is instantaneous adjustment of prices. Money prices will simply rise *uniformly*; and that is that.[72]

It was to counteract this view that Hayek wrote the previously cited passage. Hicks's argument makes sense only in terms of a "one shot" increase in the money supply. There can be a discrepancy between the two rates of interest only if markets are out of equilibrium. Furthermore, equality "must be restored" once equilibrium is restored *because that is how equilibrium is defined in the Wicksellian system*! That "there is no room for a prolonged discrepancy between market rate and natural rate" is precisely the issue.[73] The inability of Hayek and Hicks to communicate on the issue stems from Hicks's contention that the monetary considerations "do not really belong." These considerations hold together the otherwise diverse strands of thought in the neo–Wicksellian analysis.[74] The process that Hicks summed up by saying "that is that" turns out to be the business cycle.

NOTES

1. Hayek, "Three Elucidations of the Ricardo Effect," *Journal of Political Economy* 77 (March/April, 1969): 282. Lord Robbins gave a brief account of the favorable impact of these lectures (*Autobiography of*

an Economist [London: Macmillan & Co., 1971], p. 127). Hayek was almost immediately offered the long-vacant Tooke Chair at the London School of Economics.

2. The *locus classicus* for Hayek was Ludwig von Mises's *Theorie des Geldes und der Umlaufsmittel* (1912) (*The Theory of Money and Credit*, tr. H. E. Batson [Irvington-on-Hudson, N. Y.: Foundation for Economic Education, 1971]).

3. Hayek recognized the similarity of enterprise among these figures. In a letter to Milton Friedman he remarked: "We all had similar ideas in the 1920s. They had been most fully elaborated by R. G. Hawtrey who was all the time talking about the 'inherent instability of credit' but he was by no means the only one" (Friedman, *Optimum Quantity of Money* [Chicago: Aldine Publishing Co., 1969], p. 88n).

4. Irving Fisher does not fit this analysis as well as the others. His work on money is largely a restatement of the quantity theory, against which many of the other figures were reacting (Roy Harrod, *Money* [London: St. Martin's Press, 1969], p. 27).

5. Hayek, *Monetary Theory and the Trade Cycle* (New York: Augustus M. Kelley, 1966).

6. Hayek, *Individualism and Economic Order* (Chicago: University of Chicago Press, 1948), pp. 33-56. The other articles, all reprinted in this same volume, are "The Facts of the Social Sciences," "The Use of Knowledge in Society," and "The Meaning of Competition."

7. Hayek, *Profits, Interest, and Investment* (New York: Augustus M. Kelley, 1970), pp. 6-7.

8. Hayek, *Monetary Theory*, p. 54 (emphasis original).

9. Gottfried Haberler, *Prosperity and Depression*, 3d ed. (Lake Success, N. Y.: United Nations, 1946), pp. 277-78. Haberler was particularly careful to note that each business cycle is a unique historical event, and that there are dissimilarities among cycles. He only argued that there are certain characteristic features of cycles. This is an historical question, and is treated as such by virtually all concerned (ibid., pp. 274-76).

10. Obviously Spiethoff influenced all Continental economists studying the business cycles at this time. Although both Mises and Hayek emphasized the *monetary* factors operating causally in the cycle, both mentioned Spiethoff in their works, though often to disagree with him. Also both contributed articles to Spiethoff's *Festschrift* (Schumpeter, *History of Economic Analysis* [New York: Oxford University Press, 1954], pp. 815-17, 1126-28).

11. It would be more precise to speak of changes in the rate of growth of *credit*, as these were the analytically important changes in Hayek's Misesian (or neo–Wicksellian) theory. Thus, while he was chiefly concerned with changes in bank deposits or credit money, he did not treat the amount of credit as rigidly determined by the stock of

money, even though he viewed economic fluctuations as being *initiated* by monetary disturbances.

12. Hayek, *Monetary Theory*, pp. 103-6. On the attitude of the modern Austrian school toward price levels, see Schumpeter, *History*, pp. 701n, 1089, 1095.

13. See Hayek's own justification of this procedure in *Prices and Production*, 2d ed. (London: Routledge & Kegan Paul, 1935), pp. 32-36.

14. Hayek felt that Keynes, for one, was guilty of this error in *The General Theory*. Hayek at first appraised that work as providing theorists with "the economics of abundance." Twenty–five years later, he argued that Keynes's analytical framework was one in which "the whole price system [was] redundant, undetermined and unintelligible" (Sudha R. Shenoy, ed., *A Tiger by the Tail* [London: Institute of Economic Affairs, 1972], p. 103).

15. Haberler, *Prosperity and Depression*, p. 63n; and Fritz Machlup, "Friedrich von Hayek's Contributions to Economics," *Swedish Journal of Economics* 76 (1974): 506.

16. One example is to J. S. Mill's exposition of the effects of a sudden conversion of circulating into fixed capital (*Principles*, pp. 93-97). Mill's analysis is reflected in Hayek's monetary explanations of the following century.

17. W. H. Hutt, *The Theory of Idle Resources* (London: Jonathan Cope, 1939), p. 15.

18. Hayek, *Prices and Production*, pp. 36-40. Throughout Hayek was concerned with the allocation of consumption over time; he did not consider the effects of a change in tastes for consumer goods to be consumed in a given time period. Thus, at times, "homogeneous consumption services" could be substituted for "consumers' goods."

19. The durable–goods problem was of particular importance for the Austrian school. Wicksell was the first to point out that the durable–goods problem is identical with the Marshallian joint–supply problem (Wicksell, *Lectures on Political Economy*, ed. Lionel Robbins [London: Routledge & Kegan Paul, 1935], 1: 260). D. K. Benjamin and Roger Kormendi rediscovered this fact in "The Interrelationship between the Markets for New and Used Durables," *Journal of Law and Economics* 18 (October 1974): 381-401. See also Hayek, *The Pure Theory of Capital* (Chicago: University of Chicago Press, 1941), pp. 66-67.

20. Hayek, *Prices and Production*, pp. x-xii; see also Hayek, *Pure Theory of Capital*, pp. 46-49.

21. Hayek, *Prices and Production*, p. 40n.

22. Ibid., pp. 40-41n.

23. Hayek, *Pure Theory of Capital*, p. 48.

24. Hayek, *Prices and Production*, pp. 38-42. Hayek said that Jacob Marshak suggested the term "Jevonian Investment Figure." Jevons as well as Wicksell and Åckerman used similar figures (ibid., p. 38n). The

similarity to Wicksell's approach is particularly striking (Wicksell, *Lectures*, 1: 151-54). See also W. Stanley Jevons, *Theory of Political Economy*, ed. R. D. C. Collison Black (Baltimore: Penguin Books, 1970), p. 231.

25. Hayek, *Prices and Production*, pp. 41-42.

26. Ibid., p. 42.

27. Hayek, *Pure Theory of Capital*, pp. 199-200.

28. Ibid., pp. 3-13, 93-94. Much of this reflects the still very strong influence of Böhm–Bawerk's thinking on Hayek.

29. Hayek, *Prices and Production*, p. 46.

30. Hayek, "Price Expectations, Monetary Disturbances, and Malinvestment," *Profits, Interest, and Investment*, pp. 153-54 (hereafter, "Price Expectations"). In pointing out that his theory was "quite independent of any idea of absolute changes in the quantity of capital," Hayek noted that his theory did not depend on being able to measure the capital stock or (to deal with the question that concerned him at this point) on giving any determinate meaning to the maintenance of capital.

31. Hayek was following his own dictum in "Economics and Knowledge" that "before we can explain why people commit mistakes, we must first explain why they should ever be right" (*Individualism*, p. 34).

32. The two methods involve hypothetical experiments: the increase in the propensity to save assumes a constant money supply, and the increase in the money supply assumes a given propensity to save. Hayek took into account the complexities introduced by an elastic supply of trade credit (*Prices and Production*, pp. 115-18).

33. Hayek, "Price Expectations," pp. 152-154.

34. Ibid., p. 152.

35. Hayek placed no emphasis on the interest elasticity of saving. "The factors which affect an individual's willingness to save are the regularity and certainty of his income, the security of the investment opportunities available to him, and the possibility of investing in his own business . . . . It seems that in the short run the willingness to save varies very little and that it is particularly not much affected in the aggregate by changes in the rate of interest" (*Profits, Interest, and Investment*, p. 169). The inclusion of this essay in *Encyclopedia of the Social Sciences* in 1935 suggests that it must have represented the consensus of the profession, for new theories are not usually introduced in such articles. The dependence of saving on income is referred to as "self–evident commonplace" (ibid., p. 53n).

36. To Wicksell, the adaptation of entrepreneurs to a changed propensity to consume is as a rule "of secondary importance in comparison with the main phenomenon," changes in the structure of production. He did assume, however, an "adaptability and a degree of foresight in the reorganization of production which is far from existing in reality" (*Lectures*, 2: 193).

37. This analysis is from Hayek, *Prices and Production*, pp. 75-77. An application of resources to the early stages would allocate circulating capital to more productive operations. Production for consumption would take longer (measured from the first application of labor and land services). Fewer consumption goods would be available immediately and more would be available ultimately. This is precisely what consumers desire when they increase their propensity to save. If net value productivity is involved in extending the number of stages, the output of consumer goods will eventually increase (see note 39 below).

38. An investment period is "the interval between the application of a unit of input and the maturing of the quantity of output due to that input" (Hayek, *The Pure Theory of Capital*, p. 69). The concept is most applicable to what Frisch called a "point input–point output" model. For a continuous input–point output, or point input–continuous output model, Hayek used joint–demand analysis (for factors in the first case) and joint–supply analysis (for the services in the second case) (ibid., p. 67). Hayek did not give the Frisch citation there.

39. Hayek, *Prices and Production*, pp. 79-83. According to Hayek, the discounted value of the marginal product of nonspecific factors will increase for a second reason: the superiority of "roundabout," or "capitalistic," methods of production, which insures that total output of consumer goods will increase once the new process has been completed.This controversial and typically Austrian proposition is not essential for what follows, though one wonders why investment would ever become "more capitalistic" if this were not true.

40. "A change in the bank–rate is not calculated to have any effect (except, perhaps, remotely and of the second order of magnitude) on the prospective real yield of fixed capital" (J. M. Keynes, *A Treatise on Money*, 2 vols. [New York: Harcourt, Brace & Co., 1930], 1:202).

41. Hayek, "Reflections on the Pure Theory of Money of Mr. J. M. Keynes," part 2, *Economica* 11 (February, 1932): 25; and Gerald P. O'Driscoll, Jr., "Hayek and Keynes: A Retrospective Assessment," Iowa State University, Staff Paper no. 20, 1975), esp. pp. 24-26.

42. Hawtrey, *Capital and Employment*, 2d ed. (London: Longmans, Green & Co., 1952), p. 31; see also Hayek, *Pure Theory of Capital*, p. 286.

43. Hawtrey, *Capital and Employment*, p. 36. Wicksell spoke of the "breadth" and "height" of capital as capital accumulation occurs; he was apparently borrowing Åkerman's terminology (*Lectures,* 1:266).

44. Hayek, *Pure Theory of Capital*, pp. 286-87.

45. Ibid., p. 286.

46. It is questionable whether we want to measure market value when we try to measure capital. A number of writers (for example, Robert Dorfman and Abba Lerner) questioned this procedure, noting that we do not follow it with other factors, and that, if we did, some

results would be paradoxical. For instance, were the demand for labor to be inelastic, an increase in supply would diminish the value of labor employed in production (Kirzner, *Essay on Capital* [New York: Augustus M. Kelley, 1966], p. 135).

47. Hayek, *The Pure Theory of Capital*, pp. 69-70, 76-78.

48. Ibid., pp. 69-70.

49. Ibid., p. 70.

50. Ibid., p. 76.

51. Hayek, *Prices and Production*, p. 53.

52. Hayek, *Pure Theory of Capital*, p. 31.

53. Two points are implicit here. First, in a barter world, there is no medium of exchange by definition. Thus one commodity will be demanded in equilibrium in a money economy, that will not be demanded in a barter economy. Second, no alternative mechanism for attaining equilibrium is specified in barter constructions (*Pure Theory of Capital*, p. 31). See Ludwig von Mises, *Human Action*, 3d ed. (Chicago: Henry Regnery Co., 1963), pp. 249, 398-99, 416-19.

54. "Monetary changes are . . . in a peculiar sense self-reversing and the position created by them is inherently unstable. For sooner or later any deviation from the equilibrium position—as determined by the real quantities—will cause a swing of the pendulum in the opposite direction" (Hayek, *Pure Theory of Capital*, p. 34).

55. He made the simplifying assumption that the entire increase in the money stock took the form of "credits granted to producers"; this was "the case most frequently to be encountered in practice" (Hayek, *Prices and Production*, p. 54). In fact Hayek's assumption is not unrealistic, even today. Most loans granted by commercial banks are for productive purposes. Consumer and personal loans are of growing importance in commercial bank portfolios (from approximately 18% in 1947 to approximately 25% in 1970). But even for this category of loans, shifts in consumer spending are induced by interest rate changes. For the portfolio statistics, see Colin D. Campbell and Rosemary G. Campbell, *An Introduction to Money and Banking* (New York: Holt, Rinehart & Winston, 1972), pp. 84, 89.

56. Wicksell demonstrated that the following analysis is no less valid if the changes in the money stock are induced by changes in the natural rate of interest, the money rate being constant (*Lectures*, 2:202-18). Hayek at one point chided Mises for emphasizing the autonomous nature of changes in the money stock (*Monetary Theory*, pp. 148-52). Machlup was too generous in crediting Hayek with an amendment to Wicksell in this issue. Machlup would have Hayek correcting Wicksell by pointing out that a cumulative process can be initiated by a rise in the natural rate of interest (Machlup, "Friedrich von Hayek's Contributions to Economics," p. 501). Yet Wicksell treated this case as typical (*Lectures*, 2:205).

57. Hayek, "Price Expectations," p. 143.

58. Ibid., p. 141. For a similar argument, see Ludwig von Mises, " 'Elastic Expectations' and the Austrian Theory of the Trade Cycle," *Economica*, n.s. 10 (August 1943): 252.

59. Hayek, "Price Expectations," p. 141.

60. Shenoy, *A Tiger by the Tail*, p. 8.

61. Hayek, *Prices and Production*, p. 57.

62. Haberler called the class of theories of which Hayek's is an instance "Monetary Over–Investment Theories" (*Prosperity and Depression*, p. 33). *Malinvestment* is both illuminating and descriptively more accurate. The cyclical process in Hayek's work is generated when appropriate investments (given the equilibrium rate of interest) are made. Whether in some sense *more* capital is purchased with the increased investment expenditures is of secondary importance.

63. Hicks, "The Hayek Story," in *Critical Essays in Monetary Theory* (New York: Oxford University Press, Clarendon Press, 1967), p. 208.

64. Hicks, "A Neo-Austrian Growth Theory," *Economic Journal* 80 (June 1970): 277. Sir John is speaking here about *Prices and Production*. It must be pointed out that he amended his views in successive reassessments of Hayek and the Austrian school. But I believe that Hayek and Hicks still disagree about the role of Hayek's monetary considerations.

65. Hicks, "The Hayek Story," p. 210. Hicks characterized this approach as downright "un–Hayekian."

66. Ibid.

67. Ibid., p. 211. Streissler, in reinterpreting Hayek, follows a path similar to that taken by Hicks (*Roads to Freedom* [New York: Augustus M. Kelley, 1969], pp. 245-85).

68. Hicks, *Critical Essays*, p. 211.

69. Ibid., pp. 211-15. Hicks subsequently became intrigued with Ricardian analysis of the effects of excess investment in fixed capital, and his approach to capital theory must be seen as part of a general retrogression toward Ricardian macroanalysis. It is particularly unfortunate that Hicks subtitled his book "A Neo–Austrian Theory." It could be more aptly described as "neo–Ricardian" (*Capital and Time*, pp. 97-99). On the radical dissimilarities between the neo–Ricardian macro approach and the Austrian micro approach to capital theory, see Ludwig M. Lachmann, *Macro–economic Thinking and the Market Economy*.

70. "Of course, if the expenditure of the additional money in investment were a single non–recurrent event, confined to a single month, the effects would be of transient character" (Hayek, "Three Elucidations," p. 279).

71. Ibid., p. 280. Even if a given rate of increase in the money supply, and hence prices, came to be correctly anticipated, relative prices would not be at their equilibrium values. This situation would

then not be one of equilibrium. More will be said on this in the next chapter.

72. Hicks, "The Hayek Story," p. 206.

73. Hicks emphasized that prices in *Prices and Production* were "perfectly flexible, adjusting instantaneously, or as nearly as matters" ("The Hayek Story," p. 206). This flexibility is not a necessary condition for Hayek's theory, and I do not think he assumed any such thing. Even if prices were perfectly flexible, his conclusions would not change. But Hicks did not appreciate the analogy Hayek employed ("Three Elucidations," pp. 281-82).

74. Hayek and Hicks apparently parted company over their interpretations of Wicksell. Hicks interpreted Wicksell's system as being in *neutral equilibrium* ("The Hayek Story," pp. 205-7). I believe that most students of Wicksell would have to disagree with Hicks's interpretation. In any case, the difference in interpretations may be reduced to disagreement over the importance of monetary analysis.

5

The Ricardo Effect

Every fixed capital is both originally derived from, and requires to be continually supported by a circulating capital. . . . No fixed capital can yield any revenue but by means of a circulating capital (Adam Smith, *Wealth of Nations*, pp. 266-67).

THE INTERLUDE

However much *Prices and Production* furthered Hayek's career, it led to confusion, debate, and even bewilderment. At the time, most would surely have said that Hayek's reputation would be made as a monetary theorist. Few today think of him as a monetary theorist.[1] Not only did the Keynesian revolution have an effect, but also Hayek's 1931 exposition left much unexplained. In addition, *Prices and Production* had a Continental flavor on which Hicks has remarked.[2] Had Hayek's audience been familiar with Austrian capital theory, communication would have been easier. But there was no way he could have reviewed Austrian capital theory in the time allotted to his original London lectures.[3]

During the 1930s Hayek became embroiled in the controversy over resource allocation under socialism.[4] In the 1930s he was on the editorial board of *Economica*. In 1939 he returned explicitly to the task that he had begun in *Prices and Production* and wrote an essay he regarded "as a revised version of the central argument of [*Prices and Production*], but treated from a different angle on somewhat different assumptions."[5]

It should be a maxim of intellectual history that if an author changes the form of an argument—even with demonstrable improvement—he invites misinterpretation and the belief that he has "changed his mind."[6]

The 1939 essay received two extended reviews in *Economica*. In the first Nicholas Kaldor contended that Hayek's essay offered "a new version of his theory that in many ways radically departed from, and contradicted, the first." [7] In the other, Ludwig M. Lachmann observed that Hayek had disposed of major criticisms of *Prices and Production* and attributed some of the confusion over Hayek's earlier work to his readers' proclivity to frame the argument in static terms.[8] Hayek believed that he had made no substantive changes in the 1939 essay.[9] Thus, when his essay was published, Hayek's contemporaries were uncertain whether the 1939 work extended the 1931 theory or replaced it altogether. It is to this latter question that we must next turn.

THE RICARDO EFFECT

One feature of Hayek's 1939 work that provoked controversy was his introduction of the expression "The Ricardo Effect." Many evidently could not perceive the presence of this effect in his earlier work. The questions at issue are the following: To what extent was Hayek's earlier discussion of industrial fluctuations related to his later discussions? Was Hayek's argument concerning the Ricardo effect sound? What applicability might the Ricardo effect have to the modern economy? Was the effect really in Ricardo's *Principles* as Hayek claimed?

Hayek was straightforward in explaining the purpose of his 1939 essay:

In this essay an attempt will be made to restate two crucial points of the explanation of crises and depressions which the author has tried to develop on earlier occasions. In the first part I hope to show why under certain conditions, contrary to a widely held opinion, an increase in the demand for consumers' goods will tend to decrease rather than to increase the demand for investment goods. In the second part it will be shown why these conditions will regularly arise as a consequence of the conditions prevailing at the beginning of a recovery from a depression.[10]

In developing his thesis, Hayek made one radical change from the argument in *Prices and Production*. Instead of beginning with full employment and the economy in a "stationary state," as he had in *Prices and Production*, Hayek began by assuming the economy was in the depths of depression.[11] He then traced out a sequential path by which full employment is reached. His new approach was calculated to dispel the criticism of his earlier "assumption" of full employment and at the same time extend the analysis of *Prices and Production*. Furthermore, he was determined to abandon even the appearance of static analysis; his stated intention was to show how cyclical fluctuations "tend to become self–generating, so that the economic system may never reach a position which could be described as equilibrium." [12]

His argument proceeded from four specific assumptions:

1. There is no mobility of labor between industries.
2. Money wages cannot be reduced.
3. Existing capital equipment is "fairly specific."
4. The money rate of interest is kept constant by the banking system.[13]

It is the last assumption that defines the major difference between "Profits, Interest, and Investment" and *Prices and Production*. In *Prices and Production*, a rise in the loan rate of interest ended the boom and precipitated the crisis.[14] The possibility of a rise in the interest rate is precluded by assumption in the 1939 essay, yet the crisis occurs anyway.

The thesis in *Prices and Production* also allows for some specificity of capital, imperfect mobility of workers, and less than perfectly flexible wages.[15] In fact, the first three assumptions of the 1939 essay are overly stringent. Employment responses will occur if prices are less than perfectly flexible and labor less than perfectly mobile.[16] In a sense, Hayek caricatured *Prices and Production* to demonstrate that his thesis in that work depended neither on resource or price flexibility nor on a rise in the interest rate.

According to Hayek, the crisis occurs when the rising factor incomes generated by the previous expansion lead to an increase in consumer demand. In turn, prices of consumer goods are raised relative to prices of specific capital goods. This point is the same in both versions of Hayek's theory.[17] In *Prices and Production*, increases in the money supply bring about a decrease in market rates. Capital deepening occurs as price margins narrow between stages of production. But factor incomes rise at the same time. Repeated injections of money (in the form of bank credit) may maintain the "lengthened" production structure (that is, prevent capital enshallowing), but once these injections cease or the rate of increase is slowed, market interest rates rise. At the same time a rise in consumer demand causes relative prices to return (approximately) to their pre–expansion values; consumption output increases and the structure of production is once again "shortened." [18]

In 1939 Hayek attempted to demonstrate that, even if increasing consumer demand is not accompanied by a rise in the market rate of interest, the crisis (that is, the sudden decrease in demand for certain types of investment goods) will nonetheless occur. Herein is the vital difference between the two formulations of Hayek's theory. For at least two reasons, Hayek's analysis in 1939 of the case where the rate of interest may not rise was not mentioned in 1931. First, by 1939 the gold standard had been abandoned. In this situation discrepancies in interest rates are possible for longer periods than when the domestic money stock is closely tied to the quantity of international reserves. Second, Hayek wanted to demonstrate that his theory was not a purely monetary theory of the business cycle. In his 1939 essay he stated that monetary changes are not necessary for a cyclical downturn, real factors alone being sufficient. He had not been successful in previous attempts to distinguish his theory from purely monetary theories, though he had much earlier noted the differences:

I have become less convinced that the difference between monetary and nonmonetary explanations is *the most important* point of disagreement between the various Trade Cycle theories. . . . It seems to me that within the monetary group of explanations the difference between those theorists who regard the superficial phenomena of changes in the value of money as decisive factors in determining cyclical fluctuations, and those who lay emphasis on the real changes in the structure of production brought about by monetary causes, is much greater than the difference between the latter group and such so-called non–monetary theorists as Professor Spiethoff and Professor Cassel.[19]

As Machlup stated: "The fundamental thesis of Hayek's theory of the business cycle was that *monetary* factors *cause* the cycle but *real* phenomena *constitute* it." [20]

Once full employment is attained, rising consumer demand will lead to a rise in the rates of return in industries producing consumer goods relative to rates of return in capital goods industries. In such situations, it is the (expected) rates of return in different stages that influence the form that investments take rather than the absolute level of the loan rate of interest or the difference between the loan rate and natural rate. To Hayek, an infinitely elastic supply of credit cannot in the long run determine the marginal rate of return on capital.[21]

The investment decision facing entrepreneurs is one of choosing an appropriate rate of turnover for investment. In what follows one must remember the Austrian conception of capital as *"saved–up labour and saved–up land."* [22] Thus, Hayek's analysis assumes "that the labour used directly or indirectly (in the form of machinery, tools, and raw materials), in the manufacture of any commodity is applied at various dates so that Ricardo's 'time which must elapse before the commodity can be brought to the market' is two years, one year, six months, three months, and one month respectively for the various amounts of labour used." [23] Labor can be employed directly or indirectly in the form of capital with a longer or shorter investment period. Only in equilibrium will the rates of return on investments of different periods be the same.

Hayek presented a table to illustrate the effects of a rise in consumer demand (relative to costs) on the rates of return for various investments. The equilibrium annual rate of return (ignoring compounding effects) on labor invested for different periods is 6 percent.[24] It is then assumed that the price of the product increases by 2 percent (due to the rise in consumption demand, generated by the previous rise in factor incomes):

	2 yrs.	1 yr.	1/2 yr.	1/4 yr.	1/12 yr.
Percent return on each turnover:	12	6	3	1 1/2	1/2
For an annual rate of return of:	6	6	6	6	6
Percent return after a rise in the price of the consumption good:	14	8	5	3 1/2	2 1/2
For an annual rate of return of:	7	8	10	14	30

Hayek used this table as a pedagogic device to illustrate market tendencies that would be realized to the extent his assumptions adequately reflected reality.[25] Certain adjustments are implied:

A rise in the price of the product (or a fall in real wages) will lead to the use of relatively less machinery and other capital and of relatively more direct labour in the production of any given quantity of output. In what follows we shall refer to this tendency as the "Ricardo Effect." [26]

A change in the price of the product relative to the money wage rate is a change in the "real wage." The analysis is a somewhat roundabout way of referring to the effects of an increase in the value of the marginal product relative to the wage rate in some areas of labor employment and a decrease in others.[27] By "real wages" Hayek did *not* mean the nominal wage rate divided by the cost of living. He was concerned with the ratio of the nominal wage rate to the price of the specific product being produced rather than consumed by the worker. The Ricardo effect is thus a basic microeconomic proposition.[28]

Real wages may fluctuate irrespective of their measurement in terms of a unit of general purchasing power. Statisticians have often been confused about what constitutes the relevant real wage in economic analysis of the business cycle. The wage as measured in units of industrial output is what is important for labor demand, whereas the wage as measured in units of consumables is relevant to labor supply.[29]

THE RICARDO EFFECT AND CYCLICAL FLUCTUATIONS

The Ricardo effect had the same importance in Hayek's 1939 formulation as changes in price margins had in *Prices and Production*.[30] A rise (decline) in real wages corresponded to a narrowing (widening) of the price margins. In the earlier work, a change in the interest rate altered the allocation of resources only by way of a change in price margins. Microeconomists often contend that the interest rate is a ratio of prices.[31] But in practice macroeconomists often ignore this relationship.[32] A change in the interest rate leads to systematic changes in the relation of consumer goods prices to capital goods prices and of the prices of various kinds of capital goods to one other. Changes in the relative prices of (heterogeneous) capital goods are at least as significant as the change in the price of "consumption" relative to "capital" enunciated in the so-called sophisticated macromodels. However, this former type of change is generally ignored. Nor do changes in the prices of capital goods depend entirely on durability. Other things being equal, the more durable an asset, the greater will be the sensitivity of its present value to changes in the interest rate. But, as Hayek emphasized, one must not overlook how that capital good is used in the structure of production.[33]

Once full employment is reached in industries producing consumer goods, the Ricardo effect begins to operate. Any further increase in the demand for consumer goods leads to the kind of factor substitution described previously. Most important, with capital specificity the demand is always for particular capital goods rather than for "capital."[34]

Hayek's analysis does not depend on the assumption of full employment of all factors. In the model presented in "Profits, Interest, and Investment," availability of additional factors of a given type in the capital goods industries does nothing to alleviate an excess demand for those factors in the consumer goods industries; the elimination of excess demand is excluded by the assumption of factor immobility in the short-run formulation of that model. But this stringent assumption, which has been criticized, obscures the operation of the Ricardo effect in the more general case. If factors are generally mobile and used in combination (that is, are complementary), and if some factors are used in both capital and consumer goods industries, then a rise in demand for one or more of these general nonspecific factors in consumer goods industries will produce characteristic effects. In other words, once one nonspecific (complementary) factor becomes fully employed and is bid away from firms producing capital goods, the Ricardo effect will operate. Many other factors may be in excess supply, but if none is perfectly substitutable in the short run for the factor in question, the cyclical expansion of capital goods industries must be choked off.

In the process that Hayek described, increasing incomes of factor owners leads to an increasing demand for goods in relatively short supply, namely, consumer goods. Resources have been attracted into the production of capital goods at the expense of consumption output.[35] These capital goods would have been profitable to produce, *ex post*, only at higher rates of planned saving. Increasing consumption in the current period implies that the prices of consumer goods and of capital goods specific to the stages nearest to final output will rise relative to the current wage rate. The value of the marginal product of labor in these stages will rise relative to the current wage. Thus, real wage rates will fall. This basic story is not very different from that in *Prices and Production*.[36]

If labor were completely immobile in the short run, then, as the demand for consumer goods increased, the rates of return would rise in some industries and fall (even become negative) in others. As long as the factor immobility assumption is strictly adhered to, there will be unemployment in some industries, and the demand for labor will be high in others.[37] But Hayek never envisioned this type of underemployment equilibrium. For Hayek the process does not end at this point.

A single firm, faced with different rates of return on different investments, would attempt to equalize them at the margin (net of risk differences). The firm would borrow at the going rate of interest and invest in capital goods until the marginal rate of return on all investments is equal to the rate of interest. Kaldor assumed that this model applied to the economy as a whole.[38]

Hayek responded that it is a *non sequitur* to apply the model of a single firm to the model of the entire economy. In so doing, the resource constraint is violated. An interest rate below the equilibrium rate will lead to a progressive rise in incomes. The process will continue until the rise in the rates of return in the consumer goods industries dominates the effects of the low money rate of interest.[39] As long as the market rate of interest is below the equilibrium level, the marginal propensity to spend (that is, the marginal propensity to consume plus the marginal propensity to invest) will be greater than one. And if relative prices continue to be "wrong," there should be some mechanism (other than a change in the market rate of interest) that will lead to a correction.

Entrepreneurs will not be successful in attempts to drive the various rates of return down to the (below equilibrium) rate of interest. For what is being supplied is an infinite quantity of credit, not an infinite quantity of labor and other factor services. Entrepreneurs' borrowing at the depressed rates of interest in order to maintain or extend the existing pattern of investments will promote a further rise in incomes and consumption demand. There will be no tendency for rates of return to become equalized. The reason is that factor scarcity necessitates the curtailment of some production (namely, consumer goods) to expand the production of other goods (namely, capital goods for capital deepening). The assumption is that planned saving out of increments to income will be less than planned investment. Consumption demand will be greater, *ex post*, than was anticipated by entrepreneurs in general.

In *The Pure Theory of Capital* Hayek put this more succinctly:

In long-run equilibrium, the rate of profit and interest will depend on how much of their resources people want to use to satisfy their current needs, and how much they are willing to save and invest. But in the comparatively short run, the quantities and kinds of consumers' goods and capital goods in existence must be regarded as fixed, and the rate of profit will depend not so much on the absolute quantity of real capital (however measured) in existence, or on the absolute height of the rate of saving, as on the relation between the proportion of the incomes spent on consumers' goods and the proportion of the resources available in the form of consumers' goods. For this reason it is quite possible that, after a period of great accumulation of capital and a high rate of saving, the rate of profit and the rate of interest may be higher than they were before—if the rate of saving is insufficient compared with the amount of capital which entrepreneurs have attempted to form, or if the demand for consumers' goods is too high compared with the supply. And for the same reason the rate of interest and profit may be higher in a rich community with much capital and a high rate of saving than in an otherwise similar community with little capital and a low rate of saving.[40]

Lured by rising prices of consumer goods, entrepreneurs may anticipate and plan for a greater rise in the future. But, insofar as they do, they will discover that prices of current period consumption output have risen faster than anticipated: "The faster entrepreneurs expected prices to rise, the more they would necessarily speed up this price rise beyond their expectations." The reason is that "any increase of money expenditure on the one kind of good [that is, labor services] is found to cause an increase of money expenditure on the other kind of good [that is, consumer goods]."[41]

In presenting a theory of the inflationary process, Hayek provided a model in which it was meaningful to speak of the self–perpetuating characteristics of an inflation, or of rising prices fueled by inflationary expectations, or even of a "wage–price spiral." Though not developed as theories, these characterizations are descriptive of particular phases of a Hayekian inflationary process. For example, as entrepreneurs bid up factor costs, an observer within the system may believe that rising prices result from rising incomes, which in turn are being generated by rising wage rates. This phenomenon might even be described as "wage–push inflation." The superficial observation is that in the later stages of an inflationary process wages push prices up, or that inflationary expectations are keeping the inflation going. The economist, however, would know that at the root of the price inflation is the inflation of the monetary and credit media. Changed expectations alter the *form* of the inflationary process; they move the economy from one phase (say, an investment boom) to another phase (say, a relative expansion of consumer goods industries) in the expansionary part of the business cycle. But all these changes presuppose an expansion of the means of payment.[42] It is by no means necessary that this expansion continue to occur in the money stock, narrowly defined. Whether this in fact is the case is entirely a question of institutions and each unique historical manifestation of the business cycle.

PRICE CHANGES AND EXPECTATIONS

Hicks observed that price expectations were not treated explicitly in *Prices and Production* because "their day had not yet come." [43] But even in the 1930s, Hayek was sensitive to the criticism that expectations played no role in his theory.[44] Nonetheless he devoted less space in his work on cyclical fluctuations to an *explicit* consideration of expectations than did Lindahl, Myrdal, Shackle, Lachmann, or, for that matter, Keynes himself. Yet Hayek's theory is about the inconsistency of plans—about unfulfilled expectations. This point should have received wider recognition, especially after Hayek's work on the role of prices in communicating information for the coordination of economic activity. In fact, it was in a lecture delivered in 1933 on cyclical fluctuations that Hayek first presented the thesis of his later "Economics and Knowledge." [45] In *Prices and Production* and also in subsequent works, for example, "Profits, Interest, and Investment," Hayek explained how entrepreneurs are induced to make investment decisions largely inconsistent with the saving decisions made by income recipients in general. But Hayek's formal work on the coordination problem has been grouped with his work on economic calculation under socialism. It is instructive, however, to read his work on economic coordination in conjunction with that on cyclical fluctuations because the two subjects are interconnected.

Hayek was explicit about the nature of investors' expectations: "Most investments are made in the expectation that the supply of capital will for some time continue at the present level." [46] The "supply of capital" is ambiguous and suggests that capital is a homogeneous fund—a concept hardly consistent with Hayek's own views on capital theory. The point is that entrepreneurs make investments not only on the expectation that funds will be available at the prevailing interest rate to complete *that* investment project, but also on the expectation that funds will be available to complete *complementary* investments in other stages, so that there will finally emerge a complete structure of production. "These further investments which are necessary if the present investments are going to be successful may be either investments by the same entrepreneurs who made the first investment, or—much more frequently—investments in the products produced by the first group by a second group of entrepreneurs." [47] As Hayek argued in "Economics and Knowledge," an individual's plans are necessarily mutually consistent.[48] But different entrepreneurs may be led into making inconsistent production plans by faulty price signals. The coordinating mechanism for these decisions can fail to operate in an equilibrating fashion. According to Hayek, *the business crisis occurs when entrepreneurs can no longer attract the funds to complete or maintain a given structure of production*.

Hayek acknowledged that entrepreneurs may react to a rise in the price of consumer goods and a fall in real wages in the consumer goods industries by anticipating an even larger price rise in the future. They may for a time have "elastic" expectations and react to a rise in the prices of consumer goods by increasing investment for the future production of consumer goods as opposed to increasing current output of consumer goods. Since when consumer prices rise, there is full employment in the industries producing consumer goods, these two increases cannot occur simultaneously. However, if entrepreneurs discover that they have continually underestimated the yield from increasing the output of consumer goods in the immediate future, they will revise their pattern of behavior, even if the loan rate of interest would otherwise prompt them to borrow and invest for the more distant future.[49] Hayek's capitalists are not wont to entrust their funds to entrepreneurs who consistently pass up the more lucrative investment opportunities.

No discussion of Hayek's treatment of expectations would be complete without consideration of the role of entrepreneurship in his theory. Hayek himself contributed little to the theory of entrepreneurship. This failure is surely partly due to short shrift generally given to the entrepreneurial function in economics. This *lacuna* is ironic, given the theoretical importance assigned to the undertaker as far back as Cantillon and J. B. Say. But in classical British political economy it was the capitalistic function that occupied center stage. Moreover, Walras introduced the notion of timeless equilibrium, which renders unintelligible both the entrepreneurial and capitalistic functions. The roughly simultaneous attack by J. B. Clark—an attack renewed by Frank Knight—on the concept of an investment period obscured the need for theories of the entrepreneurial and capitalistic roles.

Joseph Schumpeter resurrected the entrepreneur in revitalizing Walras's system to explain economic development. The analysis of the entrepreneurial role became a possible research program once again. But the Schumpeterian example was not followed by neo–Walrasians, and there was little further development of the entrepreneurial concept outside the Austrian school.

It was to the twentieth-century Austrians that the task of developing entrepreneurial theory was left by default. Hayek only slowly developed and articulated his own conception of competition and the market as a process. As late as 1946 in his article "The Meaning of Competition," Hayek's entrepreneur is a mere shadow in the wings, even though he is the moving force in the competitive process. I believe that the word *entrepreneur* does not even appear in that essay.

Mises had already developed his conception of the entrepreneur as a moving force in the market economy in the 1940 German edition of *Human Action: A Treatise on Economics*. The Misesian entrepreneur is not a refurbished version of Schumpeter's innovator–entrepreneur, but has the day–to–day responsibility of discovering discrepancies between prices and costs and of constantly reevaluating past methods of production. He is a *discoverer* of existing opportunities.[50] The presence of the Misesian entrepreneur is needed to make Hayek's concept of the business cycle more plausible; for Hayek relied on the market system to produce the "right" expectations in the face of monetary disturbances that systematically distort expectations.

To repeat, entrepreneurs are misled by market signals that should indicate increased voluntary saving and react accordingly by changing their investment plans and adopting production processes consonant with a relatively high level of saving. That these expectations are erroneous is discovered as the real forces (the desired saving-consumption ratio) surface. That market forces dominate a purely monetary disturbance is plausible only in terms of a theory of entrepreneurship. The Austrian school (in this regard Schumpeter should perhaps be classified an Austrian) is the only one to emphasize the importance of entrepreneurship. But even Mises's ideas need elaboration to fit Hayek's analysis of the Ricardo effect. Two complex questions are involved: first, to what extent do actors, specifically entrepreneurs, learn from experience; and, second, upon what basis do entrepreneurs form expectations when important market signals, such as the interest rate, prove misleading. While these questions are superfluous to a perfectly coordinated economic model they are essential to a model of an imperfectly coordinated economy.

To the extent that Hayek's reasoning is sound, the Ricardo effect is operative even at a constant market rate of interest. As real wage rates fall in the consumer goods industries, labor is substituted for capital equipment, and less labor–saving capital is substituted for more labor–saving capital:

The effect of this rise in the rate of profit in the consumers' goods industries will be twofold. On the one hand it will cause a tendency to use more labour with the existing machinery, by working overtime and double shifts, . . . etc., etc. On the other hand, insofar as new machinery is being installed, either by way of replacement or in order to increase capacity, this, so long as real wages remain low compared with the marginal productivity of labour, will be of a less expensive, less labour-saving or less durable type.[51]

Changed profitability of different investments also increases uncertainty and makes entrepreneurs heavily discount future returns. This factor reinforces the tendency for entrepreneurs to capture short–run returns and pursue current opportunities that appear most profitable.[52]

One type of expectation formation does not affect Hayek's basic analysis, though a great deal of attention has been devoted to it in recent years. This is the effect of anticipated inflation of nominal interest rates. In Hayek's theory, where changes in the price level play no causal role, anticipations of such changes, whether correct or incorrect, also play no causal role.

Let us assume that n is the natural, or equilibrium, rate of interest; i is the nominal, or market, rate of interest; $\dot{P}^e$ is the expected rate of change in the price level per period ($\dot{P}^e = [\frac{1}{P}\frac{dP}{dt}]^e$). Also assume that an expansionary monetary policy has de-pressed i below n, and a cumulative rise in incomes brings about a cumulative rise in prices.

Yet another rate of interest is needed—Fisher's *realized,* or real rate of interest, p, where $p = i - \dot{P}$. If the per period rate of change in the price level is correctly extrapolated into the future, then $i = p + \dot{P}^e$; and $\dot{P} = \dot{P}^e$. But the real rate will nonetheless be lower than it was prior to the inflationary disturbance. The so–called inflation premium is "added on" to a market rate that is lower than the equilibrium (natural) rate of interest, that is, $(i + \dot{P}^e) < (n + \dot{P}^e)$. The fact that market participants may succeed in protecting themselves against the effects of a generally depreciating currency provides no basis for concluding either that inflation will be neutral in its effects on the allocation of resources or that capital malinvestment can be avoided.[53]

The entire Fisherian analysis is irrelevant to the present problem and is of little relevance in an ongoing inflation of any magnitude. The reasons are several, though interrelated and reenforcing. Each market participant is concerned with the market prices facing him and the expected costs he will incur. In each contract the creditor and debtor are concerned with different subsets of relative prices and weigh the importance of individual price changes differently. They form expectations about different prices, and they attach different degrees of importance to each particular price change. Moreover, the data each individual (creditor or debtor) considers are subjective, and each will interpret them differently.

Not only do market–day equilibria represent the temporary balancing of bullish and bearish expectations—the divergent views of those who expect higher and those who expect lower rates of inflation—but also these temporary equilibria are resultants of expectations about different events. What inflation premium could protect both parties to a debt contract? What indexation scheme could protect all or even most market participants? The questions are of course purely rhetorical.[54]

The whole notion of a balanced, anticipated inflation is a pure fiction resulting from a question–begging assumption and a methodological error. The question–begging assumption is that inflation is even-handed in its effects and is superimposed on a situation of long-run equilibrium. The existence of equilibrium in the form of anticipated inflation is deduced from the assumption of equilibrium. "The statement that, if people know everything, they are in equilibrium is true simply because that is how we define equilibrium. The assumption of a perfect market in this sense is just another way of saying that equilibrium exists but does not get us any nearer an explanation of when and how such a state will come about." [55]

The methodological error involves the use of the Marshallian representative individual who buys the typical market basket and is confronted by prices increasing at the average rate. This construct leaves in doubt whether there are any atypical individuals, any gainers or losers in the process. The fact is that there are no representative individuals in an inflationary process.

In Hayek's theory, rising prices (particularly of consumer goods) result from a maladjustment in *relative* prices; the result is a planned output that is not synchronized with the planned demand for those goods. Even if transactors correctly anticipate the average rate of price increases—that is, if higgling and haggling in the securities market produce a consensus—then the stipulated rate of return for nominally dominated assets will increase once and for all. Assuming that in general transactors lower desired real money balances in an anticipated inflation, prices will increase on a once and for all basis.[56] But relative prices remain out of line with desired saving, and it is the maladjustment of relative prices that constitutes the inflationary problem.

The very term *anticipated inflation* is misleading. What is anticipated in an anticipated inflation? For an inflation to have no effect on real activity (to be neutral), the precise sequence of price changes must be anticipated. If transactors could predict the exact sequence of price changes, they could predict every future price. To do so they must have direct access to future demand and supply conditions in each market. If such knowledge were possible, why would we use prices at all? Prices reflect the balancing of opinions as to future events. All the inefficiencies of a market system are tolerated because it is the *least inefficient* way of transmitting decentralized information. If the market could adapt perfectly to an inflation, then the power to choose the "correct" prices is being attributed to the market. In other words, in a fully anticipated inflation this power is attributed to every (representative) individual. If, however, the representative individual is privy to the information required to correctly anticipate prices in every period, society would be well served to pick out a representative individual at random and make him an economic dictator. Markets could be dispensed with and resources allocated by fiat. No one would have to worry about the future rate of inflation, since there would not be any prices, just allocation orders.

The conception is fanciful, as is the model of a perfectly anticipated inflation. But the conception does illustrate how seemingly unrelated arguments converge. The argument over economic allocation without prices is relevant to the theory of inflation. It is relevant because inflation threatens to destroy the mechanism for economic calculation upon which a complex economy depends for its continued existence. Inflation is not merely a technical issue, nor are its effects frictional ("imperfect adjustment"). Rather, the inflation problem threatens the very fabric of a developed society.

THE CRISIS

A typical Hayekian crisis is characterized by "a scarcity of capital." The paradox that a decline in the production of capital goods occurs because capital is in short supply seemingly delighted Hayek. By this way of expressing his ideas he focused attention on the insights of some of the "common sense" observations of the British monetary tradition of which he was so fond.[57]

In *Prices and Production*, Hayek emphasized the responsiveness of wage rates to an excess demand for labor at relevant stages of production, and labor mobility between stages.[58] In 1939, however, the emphasis was on the role of raw materials. Increasing consumption demand results in increasing demand for nonspecific (circulating) capital, particularly raw materials. Raw materials constitute the typical component of capital that is "turned over" rapidly. Users of highly labor–saving or durable machinery find themselves unable to compete for complementary factors, such as raw materials. The producers of such machinery find themselves in a similar situation as the demand for their products decreases. In short, the Ricardo effect induces businessmen to make more intensive use of labor and less durable machinery. Even where uses can be found for the relatively labor–saving machinery and durable capital goods in question, producers of these capital goods suffer. For while the stocks of capital goods can be used, they will not be maintained or replaced. Furthermore, this process occurs in the face of a changing pattern of demand for capital goods.

The capital goods in short supply consist mostly of raw materials. An excess demand for raw materials emerges because in the previous cyclical upswing capital was malinvested in fixed machinery as a consequence of forced saving.

It is not so much a matter of too much investment in money terms (or real terms, if this could be meaningfully measured), as of investment applied in the wrong areas. Without the availability of complementary circulating capital (for example, raw materials) at prices that permit a profit, the durable equipment (machinery) is eventually regarded as malinvested capital. In terms of Hayek's investment diagram, it is impossible to complete all stages on the way to a finished production structure. An unfinished production structure is incapable of producing consumption output. To the degree that investments have been made in incorrect anticipation of a finished production structure, capitalists incur losses. As capital goods are rearranged to fit a structure that can be finished, the value of the existing goods will *generally* be less than their earlier selling price; in some cases, the prices may fall to zero. In the language of classical analysis, too much revenue has been converted to fixed capital. The existing capital goods (machinery) is not all usable—at least not for the original purpose—because the raw materials (and, in the case of a mobile labor force, the labor services) are not available. In real terms, there is an undersupply of nonspecific capital relative to the amount of machinery and current consumption demand.

The crisis consists of a rise in the prices of raw materials, and labor services relative to the prices of fixed capital.[59] Moreover, the same factor—rising consumption demand—that causes these price movements results in declining demand for capital goods specific to the earlier stages of production. A price "squeeze" in the capital goods industries results. Adjustment to these changes takes time, and in the process affects employment and output.

Hayek's emphasis on circulating capital and not on fixed machinery in *Prices and Production* is less of a *lacuna* than it might seem. In Hayek's later formulation, where fixed capital is worked into the model, circulating capital turns out to be the important link in the causal process.

A tradition in British political economy was concerned with the proportion between fixed and circulating capital. In *Principles of Political Economy* (especially the chapter "Of Circulating and Fixed Capital"), J. S. Mill examined the impact of a change in the proportion between fixed and circulating capital, the total quantity (in real terms) remaining constant.[60] "All increase of fixed capital, when taking place at the expense of circulating, must be, at least temporarily, prejudicial to the interests of the labourers."[61] What interests us about Mill's analysis is his description of fixed capital created at the expense of circulating capital as a social loss, defined in terms of the workers displaced by this process. This misallocation of resources is not related to a discussion of prices and interest rates. The exposition is quintessentially macro in approach, indeed, a retrogression to mercantilist modes of thinking because processes are described without any consideration of what price incentives may have brought them about. Capitalists switch investments from circulating to fixed capital without specified changes in parameters. And the implications, except for labor employment, are not pursued. Nor does he make a connection with the role interest rates play in preventing the conversion of circulating into fixed capital. Furthermore, he fails to make the connection between the problem being discussed and the discussions of forced saving, which are common in British monetary theory and with which this problem is linked.[62]

The interrelation of the notion of forced saving and the capital structure was not perceived until certain aspects of classical capital theory were made coherent by Böhm–Bawerk, Wicksell, Mises, and finally Hayek.[63] Nonetheless, the effects of an increase in fixed relative to circulating capital existed for all to see; it remained only for Hayek to give clearer expression to the problem that Mill had dimly seen.

THE DEPRESSION PROCESS AND REVIVAL

The assumption of labor immobility that Hayek employed in 1939 was a way of assuring that shifts in demand would have an impact on output and employment; for he wished to emphasize that employment in capital goods industries depends "at least as much on *how* the current output of consumers' goods is produced as on *how much* is produced." [64] At full employment, rising demand for consumer goods causes the demand for certain types of capital equipment to decline, especially that specific to methods of production that are only profitable at low rates of interest. Demand for labor increases at some stages of production (and in some industries) and declines in others. Wage rates rise in some stages (industries) because of increasing demand for labor there, while unemployment occurs elsewhere.[65]

In his later work, Hayek undertook a more extensive explanation of general unemployment in a depression. Generalized unemployment begins with unemployment in capital goods industries. As the incomes of factors previously employed fall, the demand for current output also decreases. Where many economists today would part company with Hayek is in his insistence that strong forces in the market process reverse a cyclical decline already under way.

As unemployment emerges in the capital goods industries, the rate of increase in consumer demand, and hence in the prices of consumer goods, slows. National income may even decline. In terms of the Ricardo effect, if consumption demand actually declines, prices of consumer goods fall relative to nominal wage rates, and real wage rates rise. At some point in this process, it would pay to substitute machinery for labor. Operating in reverse, the Ricardo effect restores full employment by making the production of capital goods once more profitable. Presumably, the stringent assumptions concerning structural rigidities could be relaxed, though Hayek did not pursue this possibility.

In this analysis, consumption demand need not decline in absolute terms. Whether a slowing down in consumption demand will lead to a rise in real wage rates depends on the level nominal wage rates have reached. This in turn depends on whether entrepreneurs anticipate a higher rate of growth in consumption demand than actually obtains.

It must be emphasized that Hayek did not envision a significant money wage deflation in the course of the depression; he accepted the proposition that money wage rates are "sticky." In fact, he feared that real wage rates could rise so much that the cyclical revival would recur with malinvestment.[66]

There is more to a business cycle of course than changes in the allocation of resources between stages of production. Markets always produce changes in such aggregates as labor employment. Hayek insisted that changes in these aggregates cannot be analyzed in terms of the aggregates themselves. He admitted that there are macro variables but denied the possibility of macroanalysis; for Hayek and the Austrian school in general there is only microanalysis. To him, there are no fixed relationships between macro variables.[67] Nonetheless, he considered the explanation of unemployment to be of an important goal of business cycle analysis.[68]

Is Hayek's analysis applicable to a deep depression, such as that of 1929-33? It was certainly a period in which deflation and unemployment were fairly general. Yet in an earlier work Hayek remarked: "There is no reason to assume . . . that the deflation itself is anything but a secondary phenomenon, a process induced by the maladjustments of industry left over from the boom." [69] Nonetheless, this "secondary phenomenon" became of utmost importance in the 1930s. While Hayek ranked it as of secondary importance, he did not fail to recognize the phonomenon.[70]

Robertson explicitly attempted to link Keynes's analysis with Hayek's.[71] Others treated Keynes's *Treatise on Money* and Hayek's *Prices and Production* as similar in approach.[72] According to Robertson, Hayek explained why a turning point occurs, that is, why a cyclical expansion, once begun, cannot continue. Keynes concentrated on the secondary deflation process, the existence of which depends on a crisis (as explained by Hayek's analysis). Robertson did not treat the analyses of *Prices and Production* and *The General Theory* as mutually exclusive. Rather, the two analyses refer to different aspects of one and the same process.[73] The failure of either side in the Keynes-Hayek debates to make use of Robertson's attempted reconciliation is to be regretted.

Throughout the 1930s, Hayek opposed both monetary and fiscal measures designed to hasten a return to full employment. Reflation treats a symptom as a cause and ignores the maladjustments that are at the root of the depression. Indeed, if monetary policy succeeds in depressing the market rate below the equilibrium rate, it perpetuates the maladjustments.[74] Hayek viewed fiscal policy as stimulating consumption, whereas maladjustments are caused by planned saving's falling short of planned investment. He had little faith in either monetary or fiscal remedies as a permanent solution to widespread unemployment.[75]

Hayek treated the general deflationary process of the Great Depression as a secondary phenomenon produced by previous maladjustments. Once this process has begun, however, little opposition can be offered to expansionary policy. If unemployment is truly general, little can be said against a policy that tends to increase employment. In this regard, however, he made an important point:

It may perhaps be pointed out here that it has, of course, never been denied that employment can be rapidly increased, and a position of "full employment" achieved in the shortest possible time by means of monetary expansion—least of all by those economists whose outlook has been influenced by the experience of a major inflation. All that has been contended is that the kind of full employment which can be created in this way is inherently unstable, and that to create employment by these means is to perpetuate fluctuations. There may be desperate situations in which it may indeed be necessary to increase employment at all costs, even if it be only for a short period . . . . But the economist should not conceal the fact that to aim at the maximum of employment which can be achieved in the short run by means of monetary policy is essentially the policy of the desperado who has nothing to lose and everything to gain from a short breathing space.[76]

By 1933 most Western countries were ruled by what Hayek termed "desperados." If Hayek was accurate in his assessment of the consequences, it would be difficult to argue that the unemployment Western countries experienced after World War II justified "buying" a little employment. A rapid increase in employment, fueled by a monetary expansion, with market rates of interest depressed below the natural rate, leads to maladjustments. These maladjustments, in turn, lead to successive cyclical downturns. The cyclical process becomes self–perpetuating and proceeds to the "stop–go cycle," a familiar phenomenon in Great Britain and one becoming familiar in the United States.

Hayek's business cycle corresponds more to a Juglar cycle than, say, to a National Bureau of Economic Research reference cycle. Though two minor recessions occurred in the 1920s, Hayek treated the period as one long expansion, particularly of capital accumulation; had the expansion ceased in 1927, he believed the depression would have been mild. For the Great

Depression to be viewed correctly, the actions of the Federal
Reserve System in 1927 would have to be treated as "unprec-
edented" in their attempts to halt a contraction process with an
otherwise limited effect.[77]

The monetary shocks that occurred later were virtually un-
precedented in their severity and could not have been foreseen.
Hayek's purpose was to demonstrate how cyclical fluctuations
may occur even in the absence of changes in the "general" price
level. In his analysis of neutral money, Hayek concluded that the
only way to prevent cyclical disturbances was to prevent investment booms. His policy conclusion was consistent with his earlier
views and has a modern ring to it:

If we have to steer a car along a narrow road between two walls, we can
either keep it in the middle of the road by fairly frequent but small
movements of the steering wheel; or we can wait longer when the car
deviates to one side and then bring it back by more or less violent jerks,
probably overshooting the mark and risking collision with the other
wall; or we can try to keep the steering wheel stiff and let the car bang
alternately into either wall with a good chance of leading the car and
ourselves to ultimate destruction.[78]

Hayek subsequently returned to this theme:

I find myself in an unpleasant situation. I had preached for forty years
that the time to prevent the coming of a depression is the boom. During
the boom nobody listened to me. Now people again turn to me and ask
how the consequences of a policy of which I had constantly warned can
be avoided.[79]

THE LENGTH OF THE LONG RUN

In *Prices and Production* Hayek did not take up the question of
how long a cyclical expansion might last. He assumed that reserve losses or price inflation would eventually compel banks to
raise the loan rate.[80] He subsequently argued that even if banks
maintained interest rates below the equilibrium level, the operation of the Ricardo effect would bring the expansion to an end.
In his discussion of expectations, he was somewhat vague on

timing matters, as is characteristic of most macroeconomic theories. In 1969 Hayek appeared less sanguine about whether the Ricardo effect would check an expansion in the absence of a rise in market interest rates. To him, it was "an open question" how long investment expenditures could be maintained in excess of planned saving. The actual check might only come when price inflation was so great that "money ceases to be an adequate accounting device." "But this cannot be further discussed without raising the problem of the effect of such changes on expectations—a problem which I do not wish to discuss here." [81] The thorny problem remained.

Determining the importance of the Ricardo effect would have one tangible benefit that I have not seen discussed. The Ricardo effect offers an explanation of the Phillips curve phenomenon. The observed relationship between the rate of change of wages and unemployment occurs if workers suffer a short-run money illusion but in the long run react only to changes in real magnitudes. This approach to the Phillips curve has become quite popular. If the rate of increase in nominal wage offers is higher than expected, the worker will assume he is being offered a greater command over society's output; unemployment will de-

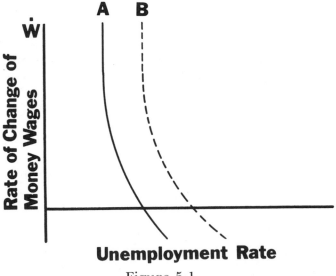

Figure 5.1

crease as more workers accept employment at the going wage
rate. When workers realize that the prices of consumer goods are
increasing as fast as wage rates, unemployment will once again
increase. There will then be "high" unemployment and "high"
inflation. The Phillips curve will shift, as it were, from A to B.[82]

The Ricardo effect provides an alternative analysis. The initial
decrease in unemployment rates is attributed to a characteristic
investment boom fueled by monetary expansion. However, the
decrease in the unemployment rate need not be associated with
an increase in nominal wage offers as implied by the Phillips
curve analysis offered above. Whether these two magnitudes are
associated in this way depends on the short-run elasticity of the
various labor supply functions. As an empirical matter the two
magnitudes are associated in this way.

In later stages of the upswing, rising money wage offers may
well be associated with declining (Ricardian) real wage rates.
While real labor costs are not identical with real wage rates in the
sense of purchasing power, declining real labor costs in the
consumer goods industries imply a decline in the purchasing
power of these wages. To the extent that real labor costs fall in
the consumer goods industries, the purchasing power of wages
paid in those industries will also decline. The fall in real labor
costs provides a stimulus to increased employment in these industries. However, the operation of the Ricardo effect at this
point in a business cycle involves declining employment in industries producing capital equipment. At some point total employment may fall, and the unemployment rate rise. But even if total
employment does fall, we would see it accompanied by continually high rates of wage and consumer goods' price increases.
High unemployment occurs despite (or more accurately because
of) the "high" rate of inflation. The existence of an inflationary
recession is explained as a natural consequence of the Mises–
Hayek theory of economic fluctuations. Indeed, it might be
argued that Mises and Hayek were talking about the Phillips
curve phenomenon—interpreted in this way—long before that
phenomenon in its statistical form had been named as such. Such
an explanation proceeds without recourse to a money illusion, a
stratagem that economists ordinarily shun.

Declining rates of increase in wages would, in the short run, be associated with rising unemployment rates as maladjustments are eliminated. In particular, rising unemployment is the mechanism that initially slows the growth of consumer demand and that triggers the reverse operation of the Ricardo effect, which leads to an increase in investment and recovery.

The point of this last section has been to breathe some life into a concept that is in danger of being consigned to the dusty volumes of the history of thought. If the Ricardo effect can be employed to develop an analysis that avoids the controversy over the worker-search hypothesis, the short-run money-wage-illusion hypothesis, the shifting Phillips curve, *et hoc genus omne*, it will have proved itself worthy of researchers' attention.

THE DYNAMIC QUALITY OF THE RICARDO EFFECT

The major contribution of Hayek's 1939 and 1942 publications is his emphasis on the details of the adjustment process. Indeed, as it evolved, the Hayek–Mises analysis became a theory of inflation in the tradition of Richard Cantillon; that is, Hayek offered a ,hypothesis as to the kind of sequential price adjustment that occurs between the time a new source of demand, in the form of newly issued money or freshly granted credit, enters the system and the long-run adjustment of the quantity theory takes place. His theory represented an alternative to the cash-balance approach of the neo–quantity theorists, in which imperfect anticipation of the price level is all that is emphasized.

Prices and Production was cast as if the market system were essentially stable and shocks were chiefly if not exclusively monetary. During the 1930s Hayek, in reconstructing ideas, returned to the Mengerian conception of the market as a metaphor for interdependent planning under uncertainty, where time is accorded a crucial theoretical position. In so doing, he attacked the static equilibrium concept of Walrasian and Paretian theory.[83] Next he emphasized the problem of the acquisition and dissemination of knowledge.[84] Not until 1946, in a lecture entitled "The Meaning of Competition," did Hayek clarify his concepts of competition as a dynamic process and of markets existing in an environment of constant change.

By 1946 Hayek had abandoned monetary and capital theory and was on the verge of abandoning economic theory altogether. Thus his conception of constantly changing conditions as endemic to real world situations was never fully developed in his work on business cycle theory.[85] There is, for instance, a definiteness to the sequence of price adjustment even in his 1942 article, "The Ricardo Effect," that I do not think would have appeared in later work on the subject. Indeed, in subsequent work,[86] there is a markedly different tone. To Hayek, the significant feature is the peculiarly discoordinating aspect of monetary disturbances. To the degree that his empirical hypothesis about the way money enters the economic system is correct, this hypothesis might be subject to statistical confirmation. But his theory of economic coordination is independent of this empirical hypothesis. The chief conclusion of his analysis is that monetary disturbances are inherently non–neutral in their effects. Moreover, *these disturbances interfere with the coordinating and equilibrating forces of a market system.*

It would be of great scientific interest if we could establish that monetary disturbances typically lead to malinvestment in "longer" or "more roundabout" structures of production. I suspect this may be true of nineteenth- and even twentieth-century business cycles. But our inability to demonstrate this empirically could scarcely count against the theoretical insights offered by Hayek's analysis of inflation. First, monetary disturbances have non–neutral effects and, hence, discoordinate economic activity. Second, the consequent malinvestments mean that there are disproportionalities in production, which in a world of stocks and flows, have to be "worked off." Third, attempts to maintain the existing pattern of investments through monetary and fiscal policy only perpetuate—do not stabilize—economic fluctuations. Finally, theories that focus exclusively on price levels and aggregate output (and employment) overlook *essential* features of macroeconomic activity.

Particularly, as governments become relatively larger and

more important borrowers and dispersers of loanable funds, it is increasingly difficult to argue that monetary inflation necessarily causes malinvestments of any special type. One could plausibly argue, for instance, that most of Great Britain's inflation in the 1970s is due to government deficits, and that most government expenditures in that country are unambiguously stimulating consumption. The changing and selective impact of the concomitant inflation means, however, that economic decision making is continuously being discoordinated. We know that the real value of pensions is being destroyed by the process of that inflation. Also we have strong theoretical reasons (quite aside from casual empiricism) to believe that production decisions are thoroughly discoordinated. The former we know from the quantity theory. The latter is a purely Hayekian insight.

THE HAYEK EFFECT?

Nicholas Kaldor argued that: "The proposition of Ricardo and that attributed to him by Professor Hayek are not the same—the assumptions are different, the mode of operation is different, and the conditions of validity are quite different." C. E. Ferguson raised the same issue: "The so–called Ricardo Effect never appeared in the works of Ricardo. It was the invention of Hayek." [87]

The question of whether Hayek invented the Ricardo effect is easy to adjudicate by examining the section in Ricardo's *Principles* to which Hayek referred.

In proportion to the durability of capital employed in any kind of production the relative prices of those commodities on which such durable capital is employed will vary inversely as wages; they will fall as wages rise, and rise as wages fall; and, on the contrary, those which are produced chiefly by labour with less fixed capital, or with fixed capital of a less durable character than the medium in which price is estimated will rise as wages rise, and fall as wages fall. [88]

Prices of goods produced with "machine–intensive" processes

are less affected by changes in wage rates than those produced by a "labor–intensive" process. Substitution will occur toward or away from machines, depending on whether wage rates rise or fall.

Now according to Hayek (1939):

It is here that the "Ricardo Effect" comes into action and becomes of decisive importance. The rise in the prices of consumers' goods and the consequent fall in real wages means a rise in the rate of profit in the consumers' goods industries, but, as we have seen a very different rise in the time rates of profit that can now be earned on more direct labour and on the investment of additional capital in machinery. A much higher rate of profit will now be obtainable on money spent on labour than on money invested in machinery.

The effect of this rise in the rate of profit in the consumers' goods industries will be twofold. On the one hand it will cause a tendency to use more direct labour with the existing machinery, by working over-time, and double shifts, by using outworn and obsolete machinery, etc., etc. On the other hand, insofar as new machinery is being installed, either by way of replacement or in order to increase capacity, this, so long as real wages remain low compared with the marginal productivity of labour, will be of less expensive, less labour-saving or less durable type.[89]

I can think of no more straightforward statement of Hayek's concept of the Ricardo effect, specifically of its operation in the latter part of a cyclical upswing. The effect comprises both a substitution of labor for machinery and of circulating for fixed capital in response to a fall in the real wage rate. Hayek used the effect exactly as Ricardo had, albeit in a different context. It is clearly out of place to call it the "Hayek effect." [90]

TEXTBOOK TREATMENT OF THE RICARDO EFFECT

Mark Blaug's is undoubtedly the standard textbook treatment of the Ricardo effect. I do not believe, however, that Blaug correctly followed Hayek's argument at all points. According to Blaug, for instance, "Neither the wage rate, the rental per machine, nor the rate of interest have altered in the case Hayek analyzes." [91] Blaug also implied that Hayek assumed that a rising supply curve of loanable funds faces each firm![92] In fact, Hayek did not assume constancy of the money wage rate, the rental price of machinery, or the interest rate. The rental prices of the various heterogeneous machines change as the quasi–rents (and hence, the rental demand) change for the machines because of changing demand conditions.[93] In his 1942 article, Hayek went through the analysis both for a rising supply curve of funds and of an infinitely elastic supply of funds.[94] Blaug apparently used the assumptions of one case to criticize the conclusions of the other! Finally, Hayek analyzed the effects of a rise in the price of the product relative to the given wage rate. This does not mean that wage rates cannot rise, though in his 1939 paper he assumed that they at least cannot fall in the short run. Rather the analysis of the Ricardo effect must be conceived of as dynamic, demonstrating wage and price changes—and employment and output changes—that occur in the course of a process.

Blaug generally employed comparative static analysis to criticize Hayek's analysis of a dynamic process of adjustment. Blaug, moreover, employed aggregative concepts that Hayek specifically eschewed (as, for example, " 'the' rental price per machine"). He apparently felt that, because Hayek borrowed a substitution effect from Ricardo, he also borrowed Ricardo's long-run comparative static analysis. Blaug's casting of Hayek's dynamic analysis into comparative static terms is his most egregious error. As a result, he entirely missed Hayek's argument about the discoordinating features of a disequilibrium rate of interest.[95]

Baumol also offered a textbook treatment of the Ricardo effect,[96] as well as having written an earlier contribution on the subject.[97] Though he was doubtful about the operation of the effect in his early article, his mathematical analysis in *Economic Theory and Operations Research* constitutes a defense of the effect for the simple point-input, point-output case.

THE DEMAND FOR COMMODITIES

The classical economists were able to identify important problems in capital theory but were often unable to handle them

satisfactorily. We have already noted J. S. Mill's efforts to analyze
the effects of converting circulating into fixed capital. On one
issue, Mill anticipated Hayek completely: whether the demand
for final output also constituted the demand for labor. His views
are expressed in his famous "fourth fundamental proposition
respecting capital":

Demand for commodities is not demand for labour. The demand for
commodities determines in what particular branch of production the
labour and capital shall be employed; it determines the *direction* of
labour; but not the more or less of the labour itself, or of the maintenance or payment of the labour. These depend on the amount of
capital, or other funds directly devoted to the sustenance and remuneration of labour.[98]

This doctrine or theorem of Mill's is as controversial today as it
was in his time. In an oft–quoted passage, Leslie Stephen remarked that "the doctrine [is] so rarely understood, that its
complete apprehension is, perhaps, the best test of an
economist." [99] Obviously, Hayek's theory accepted the fundamental thesis of J. S. Mill's proposition. Indeed, Hayek offered
an even stronger statement of the theorem than did Mill.[100]

It is a matter of debate whether Hayek accurately restated
Mill's proposition. Like Say's law, it has been restated so often
that there is danger critics will lose sight of the author's words
and debate an interpretation of it.[101] Though Hayek's restatement obviously embodies Hayek's own views on what Mill said, it
is, in my opinion, a restatement that is faithful to Mill's intention.
First, Hayek understood "demand for commodities" to mean the
"demand for consumers' goods." Second, the question is
whether an increase in demand for current consumption raises
the demand for land and labor services.[102] Hayek developed the
argument in real terms (as did Mill):

An increase in the demand for consumers' goods in real terms can only
mean an increase in terms of things other than consumers' goods;
either more capital goods or more pure input or both must be offered
in exchange for consumers' goods, and their price must consequently
rise in terms of these other things; and similarly a change in the
demand for labour (i.e., pure input) in real terms must mean a change

of demand either in terms of consumers' goods or in terms of capital goods or both, and the price of labour expressed in these terms will rise. But since it is probably clear without further explanation that if the demand for capital goods in terms of consumers' goods falls, the demand for labour in terms of consumers' goods must also fall (and *vice versa*), and that if the demand for labour in terms of capital goods rises (or falls) it must also rise (or fall) in terms of consumers' goods, we can leave out the capital goods for our purpose and conclude that an increase in the real demand for consumers' goods can only mean a fall in the price of labour in terms of consumers' goods, or that, since an increase in the demand for consumers' goods in real terms must be an increase in terms of labour, it just means a decrease in the demand for labour in terms of consumers' goods.[103]

Combining the essential logic of Mill's fourth proposition regarding capital with Ricardo's analysis in the *Principles*, and adding to the classical analysis the inheritance of Austrian capital theory and Mises's monetary contributions, Hayek fashioned an original and still unappreciated theory of economic fluctuations.

Hayek concluded that an increase in demand for consumers' goods decreases the demand for units of labor, whereas for Mill the demand for labor is unaffected by this change; Hayek's formulation may thus appear to be an inaccurate restatement of Mill's proposition. But I see more agreement between the two theories than is at first apparent. Mill stated that "the more or less of the labour . . . . depend on the amount of capital." This statement embodies the classical wages-fund doctrine. In the case Hayek examined, an increase in the demand for consumers' goods takes place at the expense of capital in the form of the wages–fund. Thus, the demand for labor falls, using Mill's own analysis.

It is true that if all factors are available without limit at current prices (and these prices remain constant), any increase in demand (in both nominal and real terms) will meet with a corresponding increase in supply. But this is a very odd case indeed to set up as the general case. For in this situation, by assumption, changes in prices, wages, costs, and interest rates are simply inoperative. It is a situation that renders the whole price system purposeless. However, it is precisely changes in relative prices that insure that "demand for commodities is not demand for labour." [104] To invoke this case as a basis for criticizing either Mill's or Hayek's theory is to engage in a question–begging procedure.

It is certainly possible to accommodate modern teaching to Mill's and Hayek's views. Mill noted that if labor were under-employed ("supported, but not fully occupied"), then an increase in demand for commodities (that is, consumer goods) may serve to increase "wealth." But this occurs only because the increased output is at a sacrifice of no other output, and no capital need be withdrawn from other occupations. [105] Rather the increased demand for commodities becomes savings, out of which factors in excess supply are hired. But the recipients of the revenue must make a decision whether or not to engage in this saving. Mill was careful to note something that is easily forgotten in income–expenditure approaches to this problem.

The demand does not, even in this case, operate on labour otherwise than through the medium of an existing capital, but it affords an inducement which causes that capital to set in motion a greater amount of labour than it did before. [106]

Hayek emphasized the same point:

Few competent economists can ever have doubted that, in positions of disequilibrium where unused reserves of resources of all kinds existed, the operation of this principle is temporarily suspended, although they may not always have said so. But while this neglect to state an important qualification is regrettable and may mislead some people, it involves surely less intellectual confusion than the present fashion of flatly denying the truth of the basic doctrine which after all is an essential and necessary part of that theory of equilibrium (or general theory of prices) which every economist uses if he tries to explain anything. The result of this fashion is that economists are becoming less and less aware of the special conditions on which their arguments are based, and that many now seem entirely unable to see what will happen when these conditions cease to exist, as sooner or later they inevitably must. [107]

Hayek's analysis of the operation of the Ricardo effect is, in essence, a refutation of the proposition that as a general rule demand for commodities is a source of an immediate demand for labor.

The reason Mill's fourth proposition appears fallacious to modern commentators has to do with two profound changes in economic thinking that occurred in the aftermath of the Keynesian revolution. First, there is the widespread adoption of the Walrasian general equilibrium approach, in which all activities occur simultaneously, and production is assumed to be timeless. As Robert Eagly showed, Walras's approach supplanted classical sequential analysis.[108] But once we move out of a world of general equilibrium, we can neither ignore the time–consuming nature of production nor continue to avoid causal sequential analysis. First capital is accumulated or saved and then (and only then) is labor demanded.

The second change coincides with Keynes's use of saving ambiguously as both saving, narrowly defined, and hoarding. Non–spending is, by definition, not a source of demand. And generalized non–spending is countered by an increase in spending (on anything). This the classical economists certainly knew. But to confound the two concepts of saving and hoarding as Keynes did is to promote a loss of understanding about other issues. This is the explanation for the loss of interest in J. S. Mill's fourth proposition.

Finally, Keynesian tradition cannot accommodate a malinvestment theory such as Hayek's. A theory in which everything turns on factor scarcities and changing relative prices makes no sense in a theory in which relative prices are assumed (at least as a first approximation) to play no role and where, in sophisticated versions, bottlenecks are largely fortuitous events, unrelated theoretically to such basic factors as factor scarcity. Yet it is precisely out of such stern stuff as resource scarcity that Hayek constructed his theory.

NOTES

1. "Hayek is perhaps at his best as a historian of economic doctrine, but his impact on political philosophy has been much more

powerful" (Kuhn, *Evolution of Economic Thought*, 2d ed. [Cincinnati: South–Western Publishing Co., 1970].

2. *"Prices and Production* was in English, but it was not English economics. It needed further translation before it could be properly assessed" (Hicks, "The Hayek Story," in *Critical Essays in Monetary Theory* [New York: Oxford University Press, Clarendon Press, 1967] p. 204). However, some of the economics in *Prices and Production* was *classically* British; these parts seemed to engender an equal amount of controversy. Ironically, Hicks was later to make the very same point: "The 'Austrians' were not a peculiar sect, out of the main stream; they were in the main stream; it was the others who were out of it." And: "The concept of production as a process in time . . . is not specifically 'Austrian.' It is just the same concept as underlies the work of the British classical economists, and it is indeed older still—older by far than Adam Smith" (*Capital and Time* [Oxford: Oxford University Press, Clarendon Press, 1973], p. 12).

3. Hayek, *Prices and Production*, 2d ed. (London: Routledge & Kegan Paul, 1935), pp. vii-ix.

4. Hayek was the editor of *Collectivist Economic Planning* (London: George Routledge & Sons, 1935).

5. Hayek, *Profits, Interest, and Investment* (New York: Augustus M. Kelley, 1970), p. vii. The first essay, from which the title was taken, was the new contribution. Reprints of articles on capital theory and business cycle theory were also included.

6. Leijonhufvud argued that misinterpretations of Keynes may be attributed in part to this same process (*On Keynesian Economics and the Economics of Keynes* [New York: Oxford University Press, 1968], pp. 15-24).

7. Nicholas Kaldor, "Professor Hayek and the Concertina Effect," *Economica*, n.s. 9 (November 1942): 359 (hereafter, "Professor Hayek").

8. Ludwig M. Lachmann, "A Reconsideration of the Austrian Theory of Industrial Fluctuations," *Economica*, n.s. 7 (May 1940): 180.

9. Friedrich A. Hayek, "A Comment," *Economica*, n.s. 9 (November 1942): 383-85.

10. Hayek, "Profits, Interest, and Investment," p. 3.

11. Ibid., p. 3.

12. Ibid., p. 6.

13. Ibid., p. 5.

14. Hayek, *Prices and Production*, pp. 89-91. The rise in the interest rate was precipitated by the cessation in the expansion of bank credit.

15. Ibid., pp. 94-95, 106.

16. Leijonhufvud, *Keynesian Economics*, pp. 50-54.

17. See Hayek, *Prices and Production*, pp. 85-96.

18. Hayek dealt with the effects of changes in the rate of increase in

the money stock, not just changes in the money stock. But since he started from a position of a zero rate of growth in *Prices and Production*, he at times talked of absolute changes (ibid., pp. 54-55, 149-50).

19. Hayek, *Monetary Theory and the Trade Cycle* (New York: Augustus M. Kelley, 1966), p. 41n. He also distinguished between underconsumption explanations and malinvestment theories. A reading of this work is essential for an understanding of Hayek's theory of economic fluctuations.

20. Machlup, "Friedrich von Hayek's Contributions to Economics," *Swedish Journal of Economics* 76 (1974): 504.

21. In the 1939 work, Hayek employed the term *time rate of profit* to refer to the various rates of return on real capital. He subsequently dropped this terminology.

22. Wicksell, *Lectures on Political Economy*, ed. Lionel Robbins (London: Routledge & Kegan Paul, 1935), 1: 154 (emphasis in original).

23. Hayek, "Profits, Interest, and Investment," p. 8. Footnote reference omitted.

24. Ibid., p. 8. There is a correction in the table as reproduced, along with minor changes in wording.

25. Ibid., p. 6.

26. Ibid., p. 10. Footnote reference omitted.

27. "We are here concerned with the relations between the costs of labor and the marginal product of that labor" (Hayek, "The Ricardo Effect," in *Individualism and Economic Order* [Chicago: University of Chicago Press, 1948], p. 253).

28. Haberler's judgment is that capital and labor are usable only in fixed proportions in the short run (*Prosperity and Depression*, 3d ed. [Lake Success, N. Y.: United Nations, 1946], p. 489).

29. After the *General Theory* appeared, numerous studies focused on whether changes in the nominal wage rate are correlated with changes in the purchasing power of these wages or move in opposite directions. Lorie Tarshis finally pointed out that employers are not interested in the purchasing power of the workers' wage, but in the impact of a given wage on a firm's rate of return (that is, the real cost of a given wage) ("Changes in Real and Money Wages," *Economic Journal* 49 [March 1939]: 150-54).

30. Hayek, "A Comment," p. 383; see also idem, *Prices and Production*, pp. 72-92.

31. For example, see J. Hirshleifer, *Investment, Interest, and Capital* (Englewood Cliffs, N.J.: Prentice–Hall, 1970), p. 35.

32. The assumption of one good with two uses (consumption and investment) means there are no *relevant* effects of a change in the interest rate. The pure substitution between consumption and investment that occurs in a schmoo model is more characteristic of a pure exchange economy than of a production economy.

33. See pp. 70-79.

34. Hayek usually referred to output specificity of capital. But the analysis in *Prices and Production* and subsequent work in capital theory draws attention to the fact that capital goods are used in specific combinations. This aspect of Austrian capital theory received special attention from Ludwig M. Lachmann in *Capital and Its Structure*.

35. In a situation of less than full employment, consumption output will undoubtedly expand. But it will expand too little, that is, there will be a "disproportionality" in production.

36. Hayek, *Prices and Production*, pp. 89ff. The implication is that the purchasing power of the wages of at least some labor would fall in this latter part of a cyclical expansion. Hayek did not pursue the matter since it was not important *theoretically* ("The Ricardo Effect," p. 242n).

37. Of the changing demand for labor of different types, Hayek remarked: "Even if aggregate demand for labour at the existing wage level (if to express it as an aggregate has any meaning under the circumstances) continues to increase, it will be an increase in the demand for kinds of labour of which no more is available, while at the same time the demand for other kinds of labour will fall and total employment will consequently decrease" ("Profits, Interest, and Investment," p. 26).

38. Nicholas Kaldor, "Capital Intensity and the Trade Cycle," *Economica* 6 (February 1939): 40-66; see also Tom Wilson, "Capital Theory and the Trade Cycle," *Review of Economic Studies* 7 (June 1940): 169-79.

39. The process will continue until "the rise in the rate of profit becomes strong enough to make the tendency to change to less durable and expensive types of machinery dominant over the tendency to provide capacity for a larger output" (Hayek, "Profits, Interest, and Investment," p. 33).

40. Hayek, *Pure Theory of Capital* (Chicago: University of Chicago Press, 1941), p. 396.

41. Hayek, "The Ricardo Effect," p. 240, 242.

42. More precisely, the product of the money supply and velocity (that is, $M \cdot V$) must continue to expand at the same rate (or higher).

43. Hicks, "The Hayek Story," p. 206.

44. Hayek, "Price Expectations, Monetary Disturbances, and Malinvestments," *Profits, Interest, and Investment*, p. 155. Hayek responded here to an earlier criticism by Myrdal.

45. This lecture ("Price Expectations, Monetary Disturbances, and Malinvestments,") was reproduced in *Profits, Interest, and Investment*. As far as I can ascertain, it was not available in English until 1939.

46. Hayek, "Price Expectations," p. 142.

47. Ibid., pp. 142-43. Hayek assumed that capital goods can only be used in specific combinations (though not necessarily only one

combination). This point was emphasized by Lachmann; see note 34 above.

48. "Actions of a person can be said to be in equilibrium insofar as they can be understood as part of one plan." And "For a society, then, we *can* speak of a *state* of equilibrium at a point of time—but it means only that the different plans which the individuals composing it have made for action in time are mutually compatible" (Hayek, "Economics and Knowledge," pp. 36, 41).

49. Hayek, "Profits, Interest, and Investment," pp. 16-18.

50. Mises's theory of the entrepreneur has been amplified by Kirzner in *Competition and Entrepreneurship*.

51. Hayek, "Profits, Interest, and Investment," p. 14.

52. "On the principle of 'making hay while the sun shines,' provision for the profits to be made in the near future will take the precedence" (Hayek, "The Ricardo Effect," p. 250). Hayek was attempting to ascertain the relevant rate of discount—the market interest rate or the rate of return on real capital in different stages—when the market rate is not an equilibrium rate.

53. This analysis is similar to that of William P. Yohe and Denis S. Karnosky, "Interest Rates and Price Level Changes, 1952-69," *Federal Reserve Bank of St. Louis Review* 51 (December 1969): 31-32. Indeed, in a neo–Wicksellian theory such as Hayek's, if i were not less than n there would be no inflation to anticipate!

54. Axel Leijonhufvud, "Costs and Consequences of Inflation," mimeographed (Los Angeles, April 1975) pp. 10-19.

55. Hayek, "Economics and Knowledge," p. 46.

56. It is dubious that transactors seek to dispose of one subset of nominal assets (that is, money) in an anticipated inflation, though it is perfectly plausible for the category "nominal assets" taken as a whole. Robert Clower criticized the argument to the contrary at a UCLA Money Workshop in the 1972-73 academic year. See also Leijonhufvud, "Costs and Consequences of Inflation," pp. 43-46.

57. Hayek, "Profits, Interest, and Investment," p. 33.

58. Hayek, *Prices and Production*, pp. 92-93.

59. This model must be amended to take into account capital heterogeneity and complementarity. Particular durable capital goods may be used in otherwise labor–intensive methods of production to meet current consumption demand. Nonetheless, either less durable reproductions or new less durable machines will be used for replacements of these capital goods. In either case the replacement demand will be for a different type of machine and will cause production and employment effects, which is the crucial point for Hayek.

60. Mill, *Principles of Political Economy*, ed. Sir William Ashley (Clifton, N. J.: Augustus M. Kelley, 1973), pp. 91-100; this chapter is the sixth chapter of book 1 and comes after Mill's fundamental proposi-

tions on capital. Of the three sections in this chapter, two (eight out of ten pages) deal with the proportion between fixed and circulating capital.

61. Ibid., p. 94.

62. Mill apparently discovered the forced-saving doctrines relatively late; he added a footnote in 1865 to the sixth edition of *Principles* (*Principles*, p. 512). See also Hayek, "A Note on the Development of the Doctrine of 'Forced Saving'," *Profits, Interest, and Investment,* pp. 193-94.

63. Hayek, *Prices and Production*, pp. 22-23.

64. Hayek, "Profits, Interest, and Investment," p. 24.

65. Ibid., pp. 25-26; see also note 37 above. Hayek was reluctant to aggregate the demand for labor, just as he was reluctant to aggregate the demand for investment. In an analysis of the process of adjustment in a cyclical expansion, the changing pattern of demand is important. The analysis would be impossible in terms of the "aggregate demand for labor" or the "aggregate demand for capital."

66. Ibid., pp. 62-63.

67. Speaking of Keynes, Hayek remarked: "His final conceptions rest entirely on the belief that there exist relatively simple and constant functional relationships between such 'measurable' aggregates as total demand, investment, or output, and that empirically established values of these presumed 'constants' would enable us to make valid predictions. There seems to me, however, not only to exist no reason whatever to assume that these 'functions' will remain constant, but I believe that microtheory had demonstrated long before Keynes that they cannot be constant but will change over time not only in quantity but even in sign. What these relationships will be, which all macro–economics must treat as quasi–constant, depends indeed on the micro–economic structure, especially on the relations between different prices which macro–economics systematically disregards. They may change very rapidly as a result of changes in the micro–economic structure and conclusions based on the assumption that they are constant are bound to be very misleading" ("Personal Recollections of Keynes," in Shenoy, *A Tiger by the Tail* (London: Institute of Economic Affairs, 1972), pp. 101-2).

68. "The existence of . . . unused resources is itself a fact which needs explanation. It is not explained by static analysis and, accordingly, we are not entitled to take it for granted" (Hayek, *Prices and Production*, p. 34).

69. "If, however, the deflation is not a cause but an effect of the unprofitableness of industry, then it is surely vain to hope that, by reversing the deflationary process, we can regain lasting prosperity" (Hayek, *Monetary Theory*, p. 19).

70. According to Ludwig M. Lachmann, Hayek observed as early

as 1933 that while maladjustments bring on depressions, the dis-equilibrium process results in secondary deflationary processes. Hayek did not pursue this issue, though, if he had, it would have made communication easier (personal communication).

71. D. H. Robertson, "Industrial Fluctuations and the Natural Rate of Interest," *Essays in Monetary Theory* (London: P. S. King & Son, 1940), pp. 83-91.

72. See C. A. Phillips, T. F. McManus, and R. W. Nelson, *Banking and the Business Cycle* (New York: Macmillan Co., 1937), pp. viii, 115-16. See also G. L. S. Shackle's Foreword to Knut Wicksell, *Value, Capital, and Rent*, trans. S. H. Frowein (London: George Allen & Unwin, 1954), pp. 7-8.

73. Both Keynes's and Hayek's analyses were Wicksellian in character and relied on inappropriate rates of interest. But in Hayek's analysis the boom is caused by a market rate below the natural rate. The crisis occurs when high consumer demand makes it unprofitable to maintain the current investment structure. In Keynes's analysis the crisis occurs when market rates lag behind a falling natural rate. Thus, at the turning point, market rates of interest may be too low in Hayek's analysis and too high in Keynes's. See also Robertson, *Essays.*

74. Robertson outlined a scenario in which the rate that in the short run equilibrates the supply of voluntary savings and the demand for investable funds falls below the natural rate of interest during the deflation process. An expansionary monetary policy at this point merely brings the market rate down to the short-run equilibrium rate. Clearly this short-run equilibrium rate is not the natural rate of interest (Robertson, *Essays*, pp. 83-91). ·

75. Any fiscal policy that directly stimulates consumption is the least desirable: "The scarcity of capital, which, of course, is nothing else but the relatively high price of consumers' goods, could only be enhanced by giving the consumers more money to spend on final products" (Hayek, *Prices and Production*, p. 154). See also Hayek, "Profits, Interest, and Investment," pp. 62-63.

76. Hayek, "Profits, Interest, and Investment," pp. 63n-64n.

77. Hayek, *Prices and Production*, pp. 161-62.

78. Hayek, "Profits, Interest, and Investment," pp. 70-71. The "steering wheel" is the rate of interest on loans. He was not advocating "fine tuning" with monetary policy, but permitting (instead of impeding) the adjustment of market rates to natural rates of interest.

79. F. A. Hayek, "Inflation, the Misdirection of Labour and Unemployment," *Full Employment at Any Price?* (London: Institute of Economic Affairs, 1975), p. 15.

80. Hayek, *Prices and Production*, pp. 89-90.

81. Hayek, "Three Elucidations of the Ricardo Effect," *Journal of Political Economy* 77 (March/April, 1969): 282.

82. The relationship between changes in wages and unemployment was observed by A. W. Phillips in "The Relation between Unemployment and the Rate of Change of Money Wage Rates in the United Kingdom, 1861-1957," *Economica* 25 (November 1958): 283-99.

83. Hayek, *Profits, Interest, and Investment*, pp. 135-56; and idem, "Economics and Knowledge," pp. 33-56.

84. In "The Use of Knowledge in Society."

85. The static quality of most of *The Pure Theory of Capital* has often been noted. What is generally ignored, however, is that this was to be the first of two volumes, the second being a volume on dynamic capital problems—Hayek's real interest. But when it came time to write it, his interests had turned elsewhere. It might be argued that Lachmann's *Capital and Its Structure* has served in its stead.

86. *Full Employment at Any Price?* which contains Hayek's Nobel Lecture, is one example.

87. Kaldor, "Professor Hayek," p. 364; and C. E. Ferguson, "The Specialization Gap: Barton, Ricardo, and Hollander," *History of Political Economy* 5 (Spring 1973): 6.

88. David Ricardo, *Principles of Political Economy*, ed. F. W. Kolthammer (New York: E. P. Dutton, 1948), p. 27. Also: "In proportion as fixed capital is less durable it approaches to the nature of circulating capital" (ibid., p. 24).

89. Hayek, "Profits, Interest, and Investment," pp. 13-14; see also table on p. 131.

90. For a fuller exposition of the argument, see O'Driscoll, "The Specialization Gap and the Ricardo Gap: Comment on Ferguson," *History of Political Economy* 7 (Summer 1975): 261-69.

91. Mark Blaug, *Economic Theory in Retrospect*, rev. ed. (Homewood, Ill.: Richard D. Irwin, 1968), p. 546.

92. Ibid.

93. Hayek, "Profits, Interest, and Investment," p. 14.

94. Hayek, "The Ricardo Effect," pp. 235-38, 238-43.

95. "The Ricardo Effect" (1942) should not be read apart from "Profits, Interest, and Investment" (1939), as Blaug evidently did (judging from his criticisms and his bibliography). The 1942 work is a virtual amendment to the 1939 work and is not completely understandable by itself. Significantly, Blaug did not mention "Profits, Interest, and Investment" in his bibliography on the Ricardo effect; he did, however, cite Kaldor's "Capital Intensity and the Trade Cycle" (1939), but as though it were a criticism of work that postdated it by three years (Blaug, *Economic Theory*, pp. 571-72).

96. William J. Baumol, *Economic Theory and Operations Research*, 2d ed. (Englewood Cliffs, N.J.: Prentice-Hall, 1965), pp. 431-33.

97. William J. Baumol, "The Analogy between Producer and Con-

sumer Equilibrium Analysis, Part II: Income Effect, Substitution Effect, and Ricardo Effect," *Economica* 17 (February 1950): 69-80.

98. Mill, *Principles*, p. 79 (emphasis in the original).

99. Leslie Stephen, *History of English Thought in the Eighteenth Century*, p. 297; quoted in Hayek, *The Pure Theory of Capital*, p. 434.

100. James H. Thompson, "Mill's Fourth Fundamental Proposition: A Paradox Revisited," *History of Political Economy* 7 (Summer 1975): 188.

101. Thompson offered a good summary of the various interpretations that have been put on the proposition (ibid.).

102. Hayek, *Pure Theory of Capital*, pp. 435-36. For an exposition of Hayek's use of "pure input" and other concepts integral to a complete discussion of these issues, see ibid., pp. 51-57, 65-66.

103. Ibid., p. 436.

104. J. S. Mill did not rely on changes in relative prices in elucidating the fourth proposition. (See Thompson, "Mill's Fourth Fundamental Proposition," p. 188).

105. Mill, *Principles*, p. 87.

106. Ibid., p. 88.

107. Hayek, *Pure Theory of Capital*, p. 439.

108. Robert Eagly, *Structure of Classical Economic Theory* (New York: Oxford University Press, 1974), pp. 126-38.

6

Was the Marginal
Revolution Aborted?

Economic Analysis, serving for two centuries to win an understanding
of the Nature and Causes of the Wealth of Nations, has been fobbed off
with another bride—A Theory of Value (Joan Robinson, *The Accumulation of Capital* [London: Macmillan and Co., 1956], p. v).

KEYNES AND HAYEK

When writing this book, I have attempted to develop Hayek's
ideas in a logical fashion, which, as previously noted, means
departing at times from a strict chronological presentation of
Hayek's ideas. In this logical and historical development, I have
noted the controversies in which Hayek was involved. I did so,
not for the purpose of entering these controversies on one side
of the debate, but to elucidate and explain his position in these
debates, so as to contribute to the development of his ideas. One
controversy above all, however, merits special attention—the
long controversy between Hayek and Keynes, and later, the
Keynesians. By examining Hayek's *Gestalt*–conception of
economics, as applied to the issues raised in this debate, one can
go a long way toward understanding Hayek's dissatisfaction with
the development of twentieth-century economics. In so doing, I
shall also be presenting in more detail some themes at which I
have thus far only hinted.

Even for those previously unfamiliar with Hayek's monetary
writings, it should be clear by now that he was generally quite
critical of both Keynesian thought and the quantity-theory tradition. It has long perplexed scholars that Hayek never wrote a
detailed and critical review of *The General Theory*. This is in sharp
contrast to his treatment of Keynes's *Treatise*. The absence of such

135

a review must certainly not be taken as a sign of acquiescence. If anything, one has good reason to suppose that Hayek had more sympathy with the earlier rather than the later work of Keynes. In the *Treatise*, Keynes was still explicitly writing as a monetary theorist; we know that the neo–Wicksellian overtones of that work were appealing to Hayek.[1] We also know that Hayek found little that was appealing in *The General Theory*. For while he wrote no formal review of Keynes's new *magnum opus,* he did outline the sources of his dissatisfaction with that work in the final pages of *The Pure Theory of Capital.*[2] He there paved the way for the never-completed second volume of that work on the dynamic aspects of capital theory, Hayek's real interest.[3]

One can say that Hayek's major technical criticism of *The General Theory* is the absence of theoretical capital discussions in that work. Hayek had earlier accused Keynes of postulating Wicksellian conclusions without accepting the Böhm–Bawerkian capital theory upon which these conclusions were based.[4] Keynes surprisingly accepted this rather harsh judgment and promised to rectify matters in the future. Patinkin has told us that "of course [he] did [do this] in *The General Theory*." [5]

"Of course" Keynes did no such thing. The microfoundations of Keynes's investment function were certainly controversial until comparatively recently.[6] Economists are still by no means in agreement over this subject—forty years after the publication of that work. Yet this problem can be treated as symptomatic of a larger problem in *The General Theory*, namely, the lack of a coherent capital theory. Keynes virtually admitted that he knew little capital theory when he wrote the *Treatise*. There seems to be no evidence that he acquired expertise in this area in the five years leading up to the publication of *The General Theory*. In fact, there are bits and pieces of evidence that he continued to feel quite uncomfortable about the whole subject, despite the fact that he had strong prejudices on capital theory.[7] There is amazingly little in the way of capital theory proper in *The General Theory*, though capital considerations are of crucial importance in that work. Keynes himself seemingly was acknowledging this *lacuna* implicitly by his titling of chapter 16, which bridged his analysis of "The Psychological and Business Incentives to

Liquidity" and "The Essential Properties of Interest and Money." He entitled this important link, "Sundry Observations on the Nature of Capital."

Among economists there is now a general inclination to denigrate capital theory. This attitude is largely a legacy of the Keynesian revolution. Some would go so far as to forsake capital theory entirely for a theory of interest.[8] At least the latter implicitly acknowledge that the theory of capital is not merely the theory of interest, a distinction commonly not made. Capital theory as it presently exists is largely a theory of capital as a homogeneous globule, a concept that obviates consideration of any important, dynamical and specifically capital–theoretic problem. In recent years, few outside of Ludwig Lachmann have been concerned with the choice of capital goods.[9] The recent Cambridge (U.K.) attack on marginalism in capital theory represents a virtual attack on putty-putty-type models of capital, in which the choice of heterogeneous capital goods is suppressed, if not assumed away. Neoclassical economists, by adhering to these models, invite the inference that marginalism and homogeneous capital models are in fact logically linked.

Of course, Keynes's emphasis on the choice of consumption versus investment, first articulated in the *Treatise*, and present in less obvious form in *The General Theory*, is a step toward capital theory, conceived of as the choice of capital goods; but it surely is not itself a theory of capital, dependent though it may be on such a theory.

However important he felt the technical flaws of *The General Theory* were, Hayek had a far more fundamental disagreement with the argument of that book. He objected to the whole conception of Keynes's system, to the very idea that there can be a theory of output as a whole, or of aggregate demand, aggregate supply, etc. Here we are entering into the most general considerations concerning the nature of economic theory. To do so, we require a framework of analysis.

Whatever we now know of the many precursors of modern marginalist and subjectivist economics, of Bernoulli, Dupuit, Gossen, J. B. Say, and Senior; and, even earlier, of Lottini, Davanzati, Montanari, and Galiani,[10] British political economy at the eve of the Marginalist Revolution was Ricardian in approach. Be this because of Ricardo's continued intellectual dominance, or the recrudescence of Ricardian thinking effected by the appearance of J. S. Mill's *Principles*, British economics especially was largely ignorant of these earlier insights. Ricardian classical political economy was *macroeconomics* by and large.[11] What was lacking in Ricardian theory was precisely a theory of choice and demand, a non–materialist theory of costs, and a consistent marginalism and subjectivism in approach. In short, Ricardian microeconomics was a skeleton insofar as it existed. Suffice to say, Ricardian value theory was at the root of this.

The contention that Ricardian political economy was macroeconomic in nature must be carefully considered. I do not wish to argue that Ricardian economics was chiefly concerned with the determination of output as a whole, aggregate demand, etc. These were the least well worked out aspects of Ricardian macrotheory:

Classical economists were not primarily concerned with the adjustments of the economy to the growth process, but with how such a process could be generated and sustained . . . . Even the static Ricardian model was concerned . . . with the progress of the economy toward the stationary state, and with what this implied for the functional distribution of income.[12]

A macroeconomic theory of growth, the macro distribution of income among well–defined classes, and the economics of the stationary state—quintessentially Ricardian questions.

The Ricardians were concerned to some extent with the theory of the demand for output as a whole, despite their adamant stand on the general glut question. To deny that the demand for output as a whole could ever be insufficient is not to deny that there is an aggregate demand. Aggregate demand was constituted by aggregate supply for the Ricardians and worked its way through the medium of aggregate money turnover, MV. It might be true that a motto for Ricardians could have been, "we can safely neglect the aggregate demand function." [13] But the

Ricardians certainly had the concept of a demand for output as a whole. Their approach was simply different from the modern one. And of course their approach was not all that well worked out, either; as a consequence, most modern "classical" macroeconomic paradigms are largely the construction of textbook authors.

The tripartite Marginal Revolution was a microeconomic revolution against Ricardian formalism. It was a revolution that took three distinctive forms: "the marginal utility revolution in England and America, the subjectivist revolution in Austria, and the general equilibrium revolution in Switzerland and Italy." [14] But these were all microeconomic upheavals.

Yet in the end, "neoclassical" economics in Britain developed as a horrible brew, in which marginal utility theory was merged with Ricardianism. Much of this development can be attributed to Alfred Marshall, who, in this view, launched an effective counter–revolution. He openly wished to save what he could of Ricardianism. The reasons for this are complex and devolve in part around Marshall's personality. But these are beside the point here.

It is not my main point that Marshall preserved almost intact the essential features of Ricardian long-run value theory, in his own long-run analysis. I am concerned more with the general Ricardian overlay that remained in British economics. Most generally, Marshallian economics is clearly not especially methodologically individualistic (compared to either the Lausanne or Austrian schools), and is almost anti–subjectivist in tone

In Marshallian economics we have the genesis of the division between microeconomics and macroeconomics of modern economic theory, because it is here that Ricardian economics continued, albeit in modified form. (For instance: The Marshallian theory of costs is more Ricardian than not.) The microeconomic approach to monetary theory really postdated Marshall's *tour de force*. The Cantabrigian hostility to a Wicksellian microeconomic theory of capital, interest and business cycle theory, and to the Misesian theory of money is thus seen to be no accident. For a radically microeconomic approach to these questions was simply foreign to the Marshallian tradition.

The Marginalist Revolution, conceived of as a general microeconomic revolution, was never completed; and it was almost immediately met in Britain by a very effective counter–revolution. It consequently advanced least in Britain, and least of all in Cambridge. It is questionable to what extent Keynes was acquainted with non–Marshallian thinking. We have his own word that German economic writings were closed to him, if the writings were not on a subject about which he already knew.[15] For Keynes to have broken out of the Marshallian framework, he would have had to read German more fluently, as did Lionel Robbins. Keynes knew of Jevons, of course; but while Jevons in spirit was against all manifestations of Ricardianism, he did not to my knowledge push the microeconomic approach to the frontiers of monetary theory. And he was surprisingly classical on cost theory.

Keynes returned to a classical, macroeconomic mode of thinking in *The General Theory*. Viewed by a radical microtheorist and subjectivist such as Hayek, Keynes's new work was not so much revolutionary as counter–revolutionary. Hayek was opposed to the macroeconomic formalism and nascent Ricardianism of *The General Theory*. His disagreement with Keynes was now more fundamental and methodological, rather than particular and technical. This state of affairs surely made a formal review of Keynes's new work most difficult, particularly since Hayek probably did not work out his own thoughts immediately upon publication of *The General Theory*.

Hayek's change of interests may also be thus explained. For he fairly abruptly ceased writing on monetary theory proper. He saw that his dissatisfaction with the New Economics (which to him was Very Old Economics) could only be brought out in work on the fundamentals of economics. Accordingly, he began a project on scientific methodology in the early 1940s, and he has moved further in this direction in his interests ever since. His Nobel Laureate lecture represents the culmination of this intellectual phase.[16] Nowhere else has he more clearly spelled out his disagreement with macroeconomic thinking as fundamental and methodological.

Viewed historically, this *Gestalt*–conception, which, to repeat, I think is Hayek's, has great merit. We do not have a consistent microtheoretic discipline. We would have had if the Lausanne and Austrian schools had maintained a natural intellectual alliance. But ironically the very figure who brought Walrasian and Paretian economics to the attention of Anglo–American economists also provided us with an apparent synthesis of macroeconomic (i.e., Keynesian) and general equilibrium economics. This is no place to consider in detail Sir John Hicks's role in the evolution of modern economic thinking.[17] But it is the place to pose a problem that is suggested by the previous historical analysis, an analysis, to repeat, that also aids in our understanding of Hayek's response to the publication of *The General Theory*.

The problem concerns the recent endeavors to provide microfoundations for macroeconomics. The results have been none too impressive so far, despite the otherwise impressive credentials of those engaged in this search. It may all be a matter of time; there is no denying the possibility. But if the historical view presented here is correct, then the recent macroeconomic research program is all a futile effort. In the view offered here, the microeconomic mode of analysis is radically opposed to the macroeconomic. A coherent economic theory could only be developed by the unqualified acceptance of one mode and the concomitant rejection of the other. The protagonists of Cambridge (U.K.) understand this fact, I believe. It is not clear that their counterparts among the neoclassicals do also. Friedrich A. Hayek and Piero Sraffa, who have perhaps never agreed on anything else before, may both be in error. But the possibility that they are correct certainly should give one pause.

This historical analysis should not be completely new to one who has read *Prices and Production*. For the analysis is presented there in a very summary form. Of course, the analysis presented in *Prices and Production* could make no reference to the Keynesian revolution and such later developments. But Hayek had said much of what I am now repeating here in dealing with the

monetary theory then most representative of Ricardian
thinking—the quantity theory, particularly the Fisherian version. Some of the relevant passages have been quoted earlier in
this book in the course of developing Hayek's criticisms of the
quantity theory. There I focused the technical aspects of his
dissent. Here I wish to emphasize the methodological aspects.
Hayek argued that:

For so long as we use different methods for the explanation of values as
they are supposed to exist irrespective of any influence of money, and
for the explanation of that influence of money on prices, it can never be
otherwise [that progress in monetary theory will be hindered]. Yet we
are doing nothing less than this if we try to establish *direct* causal
connections between the *total* quantity of money, the *general level* of all
prices and, perhaps, also the *total* amount of production. For none of
these magnitudes *as such* ever exerts an influence on the decisions of
individuals; yet it is on the assumption of a knowledge of the decisions
of individuals that the main propositions of non-monetary economic
theory are based. It is to this "individualistic" method that we owe
whatever understanding of economic phenomena we possess; that the
modern "subjective" theory has advanced beyond the classical school in
its consistent use is probably its main advantage over their teaching.

If, therefore, monetary theory still attempts to establish causal relations between aggregates or general averages, this means that monetary theory lags behind the development of economics in general. In
fact, neither aggregates nor averages do act upon one another, and it
will never be possible to establish necessary connections of cause and
effect between them as we can between individual phenomena, individual prices, etc.[18]

Hayek need have altered little in the above in order for it to
serve as his criticism of Keynesian economics. Indeed, the similarity between the quantity theory and Keynesian economics
leads us to a related topic.

KEYNES AND THE CLASSICS: THE FALLACY OF THE NONEXHAUSTIVE DILEMMA

Several generations of economics students have been brought
up on the "Keynes and the Classics" argument, as it is presented

in virtually every macroeconomics textbook. The analysis of this chapter, indeed of the whole book, casts doubt on this two–fold division in monetary theory. The reasons for this doubt are likewise two–fold. First, as we have seen, there is a similarity between the Keynesian and quantity-theory traditions in their fundamentally classical and Ricardian bent. This similarity is being increasingly recognized in textbooks, as the propositions of one "theory" are being couched in terms of the other. Thus, while economists have for a long time emphasized that $MV=Y$ and $C+I+G=Y$ are tautologies, the textbook writers have only recently begun to draw the logical conclusions: any Keynesian proposition can be cast in quantity-theory language and vice versa.[19]

Second, Keynesianism and the quantity theory (or Keynes and the Classics) represents a non–exhaustive choice.[20] As is always true of such fallacious choices, the arguer is thereby given great license with the facts. While Keynesian economic theory can be expressed in terms of the quantity theory and vice versa, the tradition represented by Hayek can be expressed in terms of neither theory. For the variables of neither theory encompass those of Hayek's theory; and the variables of these other theories do not even enter directly into Hayek's analysis. In fact, one could argue that the choice in monetary theory is between pre–marginalist Ricardian thinking and a consistent marginalist and subjectivist approach. This is not to deny that a good deal of marginalism and subjectivism is present in modern monetary theory; but so too is a good deal of Ricardian macro–formalism. For one who doubts this, I can only suggest reading Hayek's *Monetary Theory and the Trade Cycle*, or *Monetary Nationalism and International Stability,* and comparing it with almost any modern treatise on money. The best comparison here might even be between Mises's *Theory of Money and Credit* (the *locus classicus* in this tradition) and modern monetary thought.

I would emphasize once again that many of Ricardo's insights in capital theory and some even in monetary and value theory play an important role in Hayek's own analysis. Many have noted the Ricardian or classical roots of Austrian capital theory. What I have endeavored to juxtapose is Ricardian macro–formalism, or

Ricardian methodology, and consistent methodological individualism and subjectivism. The Cambridge rediscovery of Ricardo has focused precisely on what are to economists in the Austrian tradition the most objectionable features of Ricardianism (for example, analysis by social classes rather than individuals and manipulation of aggregate variables rather than attention to the relevant micro signals). Insufficient attention is thereby paid to the interesting (to Austrian economists) Ricardian insights on capital (for example, the importance of the period of production) and value theory (for example, see chapter 5 on the Ricardo effect).

There are real points of disagreement in monetary analysis. But as Leijonhufvud has recently argued, these have more to do with questions of the existence of a self–regulating mechanism of a market economy[21]; and this truly fundamental difference has no logical connection with the presumed values of various elasticities that might lead one to be a Keynesian or a quantity theorist.

To discuss intelligently substantive disagreements, one must first recognize their nature. I have been arguing that differences among macrotheorists and monetary theorists are often misperceived and are consequently persistent. These differences are not narrowly technical in nature, though the debates are carried on in technical terms. Consequently, the issues are more easily muddled than solved. The differences are at root methodological, and broadly political–economic. This chapter has dealt with the former source of controversy. The latter would take us beyond the scope of this book, though I have touched on some of the issues in the second chapter. But then I did not set out to solve problems in this chapter, but only to identify them. I hope that I have done this.

NOTES

1. See Hayek, "Reflections on the Pure Theory of Money of Mr. J. M. Keynes," part 1, *Economica* 11 (August 1931): 270.

2. Hayek, *The Pure Theory of Capital* (Chicago: University of Chicago Press, 1941), pp. 369-76.

3. See Hayek, *The Pure Theory of Capital*, p. 3; also, verbal communication.

4. See Hayek, "Reflections," part 1, 277-80.

5. Don Patinkin, "Keynes Monetary Thought: A Study of Its Development," *History of Political Economy* 8 (Spring 1976): 57.

6. Some of the issues involved in this subject are covered in Axel Leijonhufvud, *On Keynesian Economics and the Economics of Keynes* (New York: Oxford University Press, 1968), pp. 157-85.

7. On Keynes's treatment of capital, see Leijonhufvud, *Keynesian Economics*, pp. 187-314. Noteworthy is Keynes ambivalence on Austrian capital theory: "It is significant that whereas Keynes (like Cassel) was quite critical of Böhm–Bawerk, his 'observations' on capital stress the roundaboutness notion of the Austrians" (Leijonhufvud, *Keynesian Economics*, p. 250n).

Keynes's unsettled and ambivalent feelings toward capital–theoretic questions show in a letter to R. F. Kahn (1 February 1932) about his correspondence with Hayek: "What is the next move? I feel that the abyss yawns—and so do I. Yet I can't help feeling that there *is* something interesting in it [Hayek's theory]" (Donald Moggridge, ed., *The Collected Writings of John Maynard Keynes*, 25 vols. [London: St. Martin's Press, 1973] 13: 265).

8. See Harcourt's remarks on Solow's approach in G. C. Harcourt and N. F. Laing, eds., *Capital and Growth* (Baltimore: Penguin Books, 1971), p. 17.

9. See Ludwig M. Lachmann, *Capital and Its Structure* (London: London School of Economics, 1956).

10. See Emil Kauder, *A History of Marginal Utility Theory* (Princeton: Princeton University Press, 1965), pp. 15-57.

11. "Classical economics is essentially macro economics" (Robert Eagly, *The Structure of Classical Economic Theory* [New York: Oxford University Press, 1974], p. 21).

12. Thomas Sowell, *Classical Economics Reconsidered* (Princeton: Princeton University Press, 1974), p. 33. The *dynamic* problems of macrotheory were the chief focus in classical economic theory. This is in contrast to contemporary macrotheory.

13. John Maynard Keynes, *The General Theory of Employment, Interest, and Money* (New York: Harcourt, Brace & World, Harbinger Books, 1965), p. 32.

14. Mark Blaug, "Was There a Marginal Revolution?" in *The Marginal Revolution in Economics*, eds. R. D. Collison Black, A. W. Coats, and Craufurd D. W. Goodwin (Durham: Duke University Press, 1973), p. 14.

15. Keynes acknowledged this in the *Treatise*, reprinted as Mogg-

ridge, ed., *The Collected Writings of John Maynard Keynes*, 25 vols. (London: St. Martin's Press, 1971) 5: 178n.

16. Hayek, "The Pretence of Knowledge," in *Full Employment at Any Price?* (London: Institute of Economic Affairs, 1975), pp. 30-42.

17. Two recent attempts to begin this much-needed reassessment are Ludwig M. Lachmann, "Sir John Hicks as a Neo–Austrian," *South African Journal of Economics* 41 (1973): 195-207; and Robert Clower, "Reflections on the Keynesian Perplex," *Zeitschrift für Nationalökonomie* 35 (1975): 1-24; esp. 5-12.

18. Hayek, *Prices and Production*, 2d ed. (London: Routledge & Kegan Paul, 1935), pp. 4-5.

19. An explicit example of such an argument is Charles W. Baird, *Macroeconomics* (Chicago: Science Research Associates, Inc., 1973), pp. 176-80.

20. On this point, see also the editorial introduction in Sudha R. Shenoy, ed., *A Tiger by the Tail* (London: Institute of Economic Affairs, 1972), p. 8.

21. Axel Leijonhufvud, "Effective Demand Failures," *Swedish Journal of Economics* 75 (1975): 28-29.

7

An Alternative
Research Program

In contrast to the majority of economists, [Austrian economists] talk
and act like people who are doing extraordinary science. They produce
relatively more books and contribute fewer articles to established journals. They do not write text books; their students learn directly from
the masters. They are very much concerned with methodological and
philosophical fundamentals and what makes the label *extraordinary*
most applicable to their work is that they share a conviction that
orthodox economics is at the point of breakdown, that it is unable to
provide a coherent and intelligible analysis of the present-day
economic world (Edwin G. Dolan, "Austrian Economics as Extraordinary Science," in *The Foundations of Modern Austrian Economics* [Kansas
City: Sheed & Ward, 1976]).

ECONOMICS IN CRISIS

The crises are being proclaimed everywhere by pundits and
serious economists alike. When Sir John Hicks lends support to
this chorus of woes in the very title of his recent book, *The Crisis in
Keynesian Economics*, then truly something is amiss with
economics. Moreover, a plethora of cures has been offered from
various sources. But the patient must be excused if he hesitates
before ingesting any of these elixirs. For many of these appear
oddly familiar. In fact, some appear very similar to all-but-
forgotten diseases from which our existing regimen was intended to protect us. Ricardian value theory, with its objective
value theory and its absence of a theory of demand, scarcely
represents an attractive alternative to general equilibrium
theory. In many respects, of course, neo–Walrasian general
equilibrium theory and Ricardian classical political economy

share common faults; the tendency in both research programs to assume perfect foresight is one striking example.[1] At least neo-classical economics, in its dominant neo–Walrasian variant, provides the basis for a satisfactory theory of demand. Ricardianism and its intellectual offshoots surely offer no such hope. One need only examine Mr. Sraffa's *tour de force, Production of Commodities by Means of Commodities*,[2] which in many ways represents the logical culmination of Ricardian economics: general equilibrium theory without demand.[3] This cannot represent an acceptable alternative to modern economic theory, however flawed the latter may be. It would truly be a cure worse than the disease.

Orthodox economists are justified, then, in their steadfast adherence to existing economic theory, given the visible alternatives. Nor does "radical economics" offer a very attractive substitute research program. Insofar as radical political economy is Marxist, and insofar as Marxist political economy is Ricardian, then it surely suffers many of the same faults as the other neo–Ricardian alternatives.[4] In addition, the metaphysical underpinnings scarcely recommend the Marxist alternative. In a profound sense, then, all neo–Ricardian research programs, far from being "radical," are reactionary intellectual developments.

None of the above is intended to deny that there is a general crisis situation in economic theory, of which various particular crises, such as that in Keynesian economics, are but manifestations of a more general intellectual malaise. Nor am I entirely out of sympathy with particular "radical" criticisms of orthodox models. I am simply arguing that the crisis has simply not been diagnosed, though its symptoms are now well known. They have been observed in numerous recent works, including Hicks's and in previous chapters of this book. But no satisfactory diagnosis having been made, it is no wonder that the putative cures are misconceived.

The analysis of the previous chapter provides the basis for a diagnosis. Ricardian economics is an unsatisfactory theory because of its inability to explain demand or short-run pricing. Even its long-run value is marred, dependent as it is on a materialist conception of costs. In the Ricardian analysis, costs depend on "the ultimate conditions on which nature yields her stores." [5] It was from this materialist conception of costs that subjectivist neoclassical economics was to emancipate us. This Ricardian conception is not entirely consistent with a thoroughgoing subjectivist cost theory, in which a cost is a forgone utility.[6] Once again, the forgoing in no way subtracts from Ricardo's many valuable contributions, not the least of which is the concept of the margin.

Neoclassical economics represents a demonstrable improvement over Ricardian analysis, insofar as the former advanced our understanding of those phenomena least understandable in the Ricardian approach.[7] The so–called Marginalist Revolution provided a basis for a solution to Ricardian *lacunae*. All three variants of neoclassicism, the Walrasian, Austrian, and Jevonian, focused on utility as an explanation of demand and made use of the older concept of the margin to explain pricing. The Austrians, particularly Wieser, developed the idea that costs are forgone opportunities, not coefficients of production dictated by physical laws of production. Their consistent methodological subjectivism enabled the later Austrians, particularly Mises and Hayek, to perceive that the only relevant forgone opportunities are those perceived by the individual decision maker. The pure logic of the economic short run and that of the long run were seen to be the same and to have no necessary connection with any laws of production that so occupied the Ricardians.

But Ricardian elements remained embedded in the emerging neoclassical synthesis, particularly its Marshallian variant. Though graduate school price theory today is basically Walrasian, intermediate textbooks abound with confusing Marshallian and Ricardian concepts intermingled with a neo–Walrasian analysis. The classical short run is superimposed on models that preclude imperfect and incomplete adjustment. The U–shaped cost curve—indeed, the whole cost curve apparatus—is a distracting Marshallian intrusion. No wonder undergraduates are confounded by all this!

Yet professional economists have learned their early intellectual gymnastics in this environment. Probably few discard entirely the more classical elements in orthodox economics. As a consequence, Ricardian analysis persists even in the "higher level" theoretical output of journals.

My suggestion, then, is that the emergent theoretical edifice in the twentieth century—which in the English-speaking world was predominantly Marshallian at first and later predominantly Walrasian—contained inner contradictions that had to be resolved before a satisfactory theoretical edifice could be constructed. It happened that the problems first became manifest in two distinct areas in the first decades of this century: monetary theory and the theory of costs, or supply.

Monetary theory occupied an unsatisfactory position so long as it remained separate and distinct from the general theory of value. Monetary theorists, who in this period were likely to be accomplished value theorists as well, discovered in effect that much of monetary theory was a holdover from Ricardian political economy. As was noted in chapter 3 of this book, Wicksell took the initial steps toward an integration of monetary and value theory. But Wicksell himself was incapable of solving the root theoretical conundrum: how can one apply the marginalist calculus to the demand for money? It was Ludwig von Mises who finally solved this problem, by recognizing the necessity of subjectivizing monetary theory in what surely remains one of the more neglected works of monetary theory.[8] Curiously, though, he is accused of perpetuating the very problem that he solved.[9]

By building on the foundations laid by Mises, and indirectly by Wicksell, Hayek provided a microfoundation for monetary theory. He did so by showing that monetary theory could be viewed as an extension of the barter theory of price, rather than approached macroeconomically in the Ricardian tradition. For Hayek, the *quaesitum* of monetary theory is not the determination of the value of money, but the determination of the effects of monetary disturbances on (relative) prices and production. Moreover, Hayek's microfoundations and his general theoretical approach are independent of his specific empirical hypothesis about precisely how monetary disturbances typically operate. That is, the approach can be readily adopted to changing institutional arrangements (for example, the increasing role of government expenditures) and thus take account of changing consequences for the real sector of monetary disturbances.

Keynes was a comparatively late convert to these changes in monetary theory. Perhaps the reason was that he could never slough off entirely his Marshallian epidermis. Or, perhaps, as Mrs. Robinson now claims, Keynes did not at all times fully comprehend the point of his own revolution.[10] In any case, he was never fully successful in articulating the centrality of *relative* prices in any monetary explanation of cyclical fluctuations.[11]

Hayek worked out the fundamentals of the problem in much more detail. This is most obvious in the case of the analysis of investment demand, but it is even more true in his analysis of prices as signaling devices and the role of changes in the array of relative prices on entrepreneurial expectations. In this regard, Hayek always treated changes in expectations as endogenous, whereas Keynes saw them more as an exogenous element in the market system.

The second area of concern was cost and supply theory. This area involved a number of problems, related by the common element of an ill–defined cost theory. The literature is too vast and diverse to cite here, but it covered such problems as the relation between costs and supply and the disappearing supply curve in monopoly. The aspect of this general problem that interests us here is the question whether opportunity costs are subjective or objective in nature. Hayek's interest in this issue can be seen as one with his interest in monetary questions. He wanted to develop a consistently methodological individualist and subjectivist theory of the coordination of economic activities. It would not do to leave cost theory hanging in the air, as it were, borrowed from Ricardian economics. The problems with inherited cost theory become apparent in the Socialist-calculation debate. Costs are not data for the individual, given to him as they are to the economist as ideal observer who constructs the models of decision making. Different transactors have different perceptions of the data and acquire different bits of knowledge about relevant opportunities. Moreover, even if all individuals, *mirabile dictu*, had the same experiences, they would interpret these differently. It is as if each of us saw part of some production function. Even if some central allocator costlessly and instantaneously collected all our perceptions as they occurred, he would discover that they did not make up one common production function. If perceived opportunities differ, the criterion of allocating according to costs—as though costs were a unique and measurable magnitude—is seen as non–operational, illusory, and, hence, irrelevant.[12]

All of these issues were actively discussed and debated in the thirties. Though surely no part of his intention, what Keynes did in *The General Theory* was to direct attention away from these central theoretical questions. Whatever *The General Theory* may have taught us, it answered none of these questions. Rather, the Keynesian revolution diverted attention away from these questions and effectively closed off paths of inquiry that at the time evidenced every sign of leading to a solution.

My argument, then, is that the various crises in economics are manifestations of inconsistencies in the neoclassical research program. These inconsistencies are present because of the curious admixture of Ricardianism and neoclassicism present in the modern research program. The inconsistencies were never resolved, though their resolution was in sight in the thirties when it was aborted by the Keynesian revolution. The current situation is the result of forty years of repressed debate over the very fundamental questions that occupied economists in the earlier period. We are now condemned to relive the debates unless we succeed in using the earlier discussion as starting points.

In particular, Mises and Hayek went a long way toward solving a theoretical problem that besets economists today—the integration of monetary and value theory. Whatever else can be said about Hayek's monetary economics, his work does consist of a monetary theory erected upon a consistent microfoundation. Whatever else can be said about almost any other monetary theory of economic fluctuations, it lacks that consistency. Since an avowed purpose of macro and monetary theory today is to provide a microfoundation for the analysis of economic fluctuations, this alone recommends a reconsideration of Hayek's work. It is true that an acceptance of his approach involves abandoning some of what is presently taken for granted (for example, monetary theory is the determination of the value of money).

But once one accepts the fact that something is not quite right with the grand neoclassical synthesis, one is virtually committed to abandoning something substantial in the orthodox research program. The only question is what.

A HAYEKIAN RESEARCH PROGRAM

It would be to go far beyond the scope of this book to outline in detail a new Austrian or Hayekian research program. Such a program is really only in the first stage of development.[13] This is partly because Hayek's attention turned elsewhere at a crucial moment, and because the Keynesian revolution swept aside many of the interesting questions that would surely be addressed in such a research program. In a very real sense, the program will be whatever those who choose to work in a Hayekian framework make it.

Above all else, Hayek emphasized a microeconomic approach to economic questions. Conventional macroeconomic models with constant functional relationships that can be mechanically manipulated are virtually ruled out of such a program.[14] It is doubtful that there can ever be a Hayekian alternative to the Hicksian cross.[15] This is true, not because Hayek's theory is needlessly complex, but because the world is too complex to picture it accurately in simplistic formulae. So long as economists are wedded to the contrary idea, so long will progress in the theory of economic fluctuations be stalled. In this, I should say, there is affinity between Hayek's views and those of Professor G. L. S. Shackle and the other Keynesians who agree with Shackle's radical interpretation of Keynes.[16]

Conversely, one area that seemingly cries out for attention is the sequence of effects in an inflationary expansion. Here one must distinguish carefully between Hayek's theory of economic fluctuations and his empirical hypotheses concerning the effects of an inflation of the money stock. His theory is in the Cantillon tradition, which, broadly speaking, emphasizes distribution effects. Hayek's hypothesis concerns where and how injections of money and credit enter the economy. He looked to private investment as the key variable. It would not be surprising if since 1931 there had been important changes in the paths taken in the inflation process. As an example, federal spending is a much more important part of the economy than it was in 1931. A substantial part of increases in the money stock, broadly or narrowly defined, is typically due to monetization of the debt. What is the net effect of government spending on the "consumption–investment" ratio? Does it stimulate investment or consumption relatively more? And particular kinds of private investment more than others? Do particular sectors, industries, or even firms usually gain first in such an inflation? These are the kinds of questions that will undoubtedly be addressed in a Hayekian research program in monetary theory.[17]

Finally, on the most general level a Hayekian research program must surely be concerned with the coordination of economic activities and the emergence of an undesigned ("spontaneous") order.[18]

WHERE ARE THE AUSTRIANS NOW?

Hayek recently commented: "But though there is no longer a distinct Austrian School, I believe there is still a distinct Austrian tradition from which we may hope for many further contributions to the future development of economic theory." [19]

There certainly are areas in which Hayek and his fellow economists have had an identifiable impact on current economic thought. One could scarcely call orthodox cost theory "Austrian," but some versions contain strong Austrian elements. As James Buchanan has argued, there is really a separate and distinct approach to cost theory, in which the subjective element is strongly emphasized.[20] Though never incorporated entirely into orthodox economic theory as such, this approach, heavily influenced by the twentieth-century Austrians, represents a lively alternative.

Elements of Austrian capital theory have been incorporated into many theoretical discussions about capital—especially in the period of investment approach. One could argue, of course, that other *essential* features of Austrian capital theory (for example, its emphasis on time preference and the subjective factors) are missing in these contemporary treatments. Yet Austrian capital theory, too, has been kept alive as an independent approach, though little has been done with it since World War II. [21]

A sort of modern version of the Austrian school is apparently emerging. In periods of intellectual convergence, such as we have had since the Keynesian research program was developed, there is comparatively little scope for distinct schools in a science. In periods of intellectual divergence, in which we now appear to be, there is comparatively more scope for fundamental disagreement and for distinct schools of thought.[22] A number of new articles and books have been written in this emergent school. [23] There is every indication that once again the intellectual climate exists in which the theoretical conundrums can be solved; and economists who consider themselves as part of the Austrian tradition will be addressing themselves to the pressing theoretical and practical problems of the day. Economics can only gain from this development, for in intellectual endeavors, too, increased competition is beneficial.

NOTES

1. The theoretical connection between Ricardian classical political economy and Walrasian neoclassical economics has been recently noted by Robert Eagly: "Janus–like, the Walrasian system is situated between two great systems of economic theory. It forms the capstone to classical theory on the one side, and on the other the cornerstone to the modern post–classical theory. It provided answers to questions posed by the normal progression of theoretical inquiry within the classical framework. But at the same time it posed new questions that were to occupy the attention and time of economists during the following century" (Eagly, *Structure of Classical Economic Theory* [New York: Oxford University Press, 1974], p. 134).

2. New York: Cambridge University Press, 1960.

3. Nuti has recently characterized the approach of Sraffa and others as "a general equilibrium approach with the preference side chopped off." And he argued that "the approach . . . has no overwhelming advantages over the general equilibrium approach" (Dominco

Mario Nuti, "On the Rates of Return on Investment," *Kyklos* 27 [1974]:
357). Nuti likewise identifies the Sraffa approach as " 'classical' " (Nuti,
357-58).

4. The term "Neo–Ricardian" is borrowed from L. M. Lachmann,
Macro–economic Thinking and the Market Economy (London: The Institute
of Economic Affairs, 1973).

5. Philip H. Wicksteed, "The Scope and Method of Political
Economy," in *Readings in Price Theory*, George J. Stigler and Kenneth E.
Boulding, eds., (Homewood, Ill.: Richard D. Irwin, 1952), p. 19n.

6. Recent works articulating this view are James M. Buchanan, *Cost
and Choice* (Chicago: Markham Publishing Co., 1969); and James M.
Buchanan and G. F. Thirlby, eds., *L.S.E. Essays on Cost* (London:
Weidenfield Nicolsen, 1973).

7. Leijonhufvud has recently made a persuasive case that the use of
"neoclassical" is more confusing than illuminating. As much separated
the " 'neoclassical' grants" as bound them together. He argued that we
dispense entirely with the term. See Axel Leijonhufvud, "The Varieties
of Price Theory: What Microfoundations for Macrotheory?" U.C.L.A.
Discussion Paper Number 44 (Los Angeles: mimeographed, 1974).
William Jaffé has taken up the same theme recently in "Menger,
Jevons, and Walras De–Homogenized," *Economic Inquiry* 14 (December
1976):511-24. In my defense, I would note that I have tried to limit the
use of the term to those cases where the similarities of the various
neoclassical schools are greatest. I recognize, however, that these
similarities have been greatly exaggerated in recent years.

8. Mises, *Theory of Money and Credit*, new ed., trans. H. E. Batson
(Irvington-on-Hudson, N. Y.: The Foundation for Economic Education, 1971).

9. See Don Patinkin, *Money, Interest, and Prices*, 2d ed. (New York:
Harper & Row, 1965), pp. 79, 574-75.

10. See Joan Robinson, "What Has Become of the Keynesian Revolution?" in *Essays on John Maynard Keynes,* ed., Milo Keynes (New York:
Cambridge University Press, 1975), p. 125.

11. See Axel Leijonhufvud, *On Keynesian Economics and the Economics
of Keynes* (New York: Oxford University Press, 1968), p. 24. On the
other hand, Patinkin apparently sees little role for changes in relative
prices in Keynes's theoretical vision. (Don Patinkin, "Keynes' Monetary
Thought," *History of Political Economy* 8 [Spring 1976], 45).

12. For the methodological subjectivist, it is an essential feature of
human affairs that this be so. And the social scientist must take account
of this, as Hayek long ago noted: "In the social sciences the things are
what people think they are. Money is money, a word is a word, a
cosmetic is a cosmetic, if and because somebody thinks they are" ("The
Facts of the Social Sciences," in *Individualism and Economics Order*
[Chicago: University of Chicago Press, 1948], p. 60).

13. Some papers in this development appear in Edwin G. Dolan, ed., *The Foundations of Modern Austrian Economics* (Kansas City: Sheed & Ward, 1976). More will appear in a forthcoming proceedings of a conference on Austrian Economic Theory held at Windsor Castle in 1976.

14. See Hayek, "Personal Recollections of Keynes," in *A Tiger by the Tail*, ed. Sudha R. Shenoy (London: Institute of Economic Affairs, 1972), pp. 101-2.

15. On this, see Roger Garrison's, "Austrian Macroeconomies," a paper prepared for the 1976 Symposium on Austrian Economics at Windsor Castle (Menlo Park, Calif., 1976). Forthcoming.

16. For a synopsis of Shackle's views, see his "Keynes and Today's Establishment in Economic Theory: A View," *Journal of Economic Literature* 11 (June 1973): 516-19.

17. The American Geographical Society is currently engaged in a study of the *spatial* diffusion of inflation in the United States. This is very much a topic of the kind that I am discussing.

18. See Gerald P. O'Driscoll, Jr., "Spontaneous Order and the Coordination of Economic Activities," a paper prepared for the 1976 Symposium on Austrian Economics at Windsor Castle (Menlo Park, Calif., 1976). Forthcoming.

19. Hayek, "The Place of Menger's *Grundsätze* in the History of Economic Thought," in *Carl Menger and the Austrian School of Economics*, J. R. Hicks and W. Weber, eds. (Oxford: Oxford University Press, The Clarendon Press, 1973), p. 13.

20. See the references cited in note 6.

21. Two works written in this tradition are Ludwig M. Lachmann, *Capital and its Structure* (London: London School of Economics, 1956); and Israel M. Kirzner, *An Essay on Capital* (New York: Augustus M. Kelley, 1966).

22. Professor Lachmann first offered this analysis in a talk at the University of Delaware in June 1976.

23. Some of these can be found in the seected bibliography of the Dolan book cited in note 13.

Bibliography

Abramovitz, Moses, et al. *The Allocation of Economic Resources*. Stanford, Calif.: Stanford University Press, 1959.

Alchian, Armen A., and Allen, William R. *University Economics*. 3d ed. Belmont, Calif.: Wadsworth Publishing Co., 1972.

Allen, R. G. D. "A Reconsideration of the Theory of Value." Part 2. *Economica*, n.s. 1 (May 1934):196-219.

Baumol, William J. *Economic Theory and Operations Research*. 2d ed. Englewood Cliffs, N.J.: Prentice-Hall, 1965.

Black, R. D. Collison; Coats, A. W.; and Goodwin, Craufurd D. W., eds. *The Marginal Revolution in Economics*. Durham, N.C.: Duke University Press, 1973.

Blaug, Mark. *Economic Theory in Retrospect*. Rev. ed. Homewood, Ill.: Richard D. Irwin, 1968.

————. "Kuhn Versus Lakatos, or Paradigms Versus Research Programmes in the History of Economics." *History of Political Economy* 7 (Winter 1975):399-433.

Böhm-Bawerk, Eugen von. *Capital and Interest*. Translated by George D. Huncke, and Hans F. Sennholz. South Holland, Ill.: Libertarian Press, 1959.

Brozen, Yale M. "The Antitrust Task Force Deconcentration Recommendation." *Journal of Law & Economics* 13 (October 1970):279-92.

Buchanan, James M. *Cost and Choice*. Chicago: Markham Publishing Co., 1969.

Buchanan, James M., and Thirlby, G. F., eds. *L.S.E. Essays on Cost*. London: Weidenfield Nicolsen, 1973.

Buechner, M. Northrup. "Frank Knight on Capital as the Only Factor of Production." *Journal of Economic Issues* 10 (September 1967):598-617.

Campbell, Colin D., and Campbell, Rosemary G. *An Introduction to Money and Banking*. New York: Holt, Rinehart & Winston, 1972.

Cheung, Steven N. S. "Transactions Cost, Risk Aversion, and the Choice of Contractual Arrangements." *Journal of Law & Economics* 12 (April 1969):23-42.

———. "The Structure of a Contract and the Theory of a Non–exclusive Resource." *Journal of Law & Economics* 13 (April 1970):49-70.

Clower, R. W., ed. *Monetary Theory*. Baltimore: Penguin Books, 1970.

Clower, Robert W., and Due, John F. *Microeconomics*. 6th ed. Homewood, Ill.: Richard D. Irwin, 1972.

Davis, J. Ronnie. "Henry Simons, the Radical: Some Documentary Evidence." *History of Political Economy* 1 (Fall 1969):388-94.

———. *The New Economics and the Old Economists*. Ames, Ia.: Iowa State University Press, 1971.

Dolan, Edwin G., ed. *The Foundations of Modern Austrian Economics*. Kansas City: Sheed & Ward, 1976.

Dunlap, J. T. "The Movement of Real and Money Wage Rates." *Economic Journal* 48 (September 1938):413-34.

Eagly, Robert V. *The Structure of Classical Economic Theory*. New York: Oxford University Press, 1974.

Eisner, Robert. "On Growth Models and the Neo–Classical Resurgence." *Economic Journal* 78 (December 1968):707-21.

Ferguson, C. E. "The Specialization Gap: Barton, Ricardo, and Hollander." *History of Political Economy* 5 (Spring 1973):1-13.

Fetter, Frank W. "The Relation of Economic Thought to Economic History," *American Economic Review* 55 (May 1965):136-42.

Fisher, Irving. "The Business Cycle Largely a 'Dance of the Dollar'." *Journal of the American Statistical Association* 18 (1922-23):1024-28.

Friedman, Milton. *The Optimum Quantity of Money*. Chicago: Aldine Publishing Co., 1969.

———. "A Theoretical Framework for Monetary Analysis." *Journal of Political Economy* 78 (March/April 1970):193-238.

———. "A Monetary Theory of Nominal Income." *Journal of Political Economy* 79 (March/April 1971):323-37.

———. "Comments on the Critics." *Journal of Political Economy* 80 (September/October 1972):906-50.

———. ed. *Studies in the Quantity Theory of Money*. Chicago: University of Chicago Press, 1956.

Garrison, Roger. "Austrian Macroeconomics." Menlo Park, Calif.: Photocopy, 1976.

Grossman, Hershel I. "Was Keynes a 'Keynesian'?" *Journal of Economic Literature* 10 (March 1972):26-30.

Haberler, Gottfried. *Prosperity and Depression*. 3d ed. Lake Success, N.Y.: United Nations, 1946.

Hansen, Alvin, and Tout, Herbert. "Annual Survey of the Business Cycle Theory: Investment and Saving in Business Cycle Theory." *Econometrica* 1 (April 1933):119-47.

Harrod, Roy. *Money*. London: St. Martin's Press, 1969.

Hawtrey, Ralph G. "The Trade Cycle and Capital Intensity." *Economica*, n.s. 7 (February 1940):1-15.

———. "Professor Hayek's Pure Theory of Capital." *Economic Journal* 51 (June–September 1941):281-90.

———. *Capital and Employment*. 2d ed. London: Longmans, Green & Co., 1952.

Hayek, Friedrich A. "Reflections on the Pure Theory of Money of Mr. J. M. Keynes." Part 1. *Economica* 11 (August 1931):270-95.

———. "A Rejoinder."*Economica* 11 (November 1931):398-403.

———. "Reflections on the Pure Theory of Money of Mr. J. M. Keynes." Part 2. *Economica* 12 (February 1932):22-44.

———. "Money and Capital: A Reply." *Economic Journal* 42 (June 1932):237-49.

———. "The Trend of Economic Thinking." *Economica* 13 (1933):121-37.

———. *Monetary Theory and the Trade Cycle*. 1933 Reprint. Translated by N. Kaldor and H. M. Croome. New York: Augustus M. Kelley, 1966.

———. *Prices and Production*. 2d ed. London: Routledge & Kegan Paul, 1935.

———. *Profits, Interest, and Investment*. 1939 Reprint. New York: Augustus M. Kelley, 1970.

———. *The Pure Theory of Capital*. Chicago: University of Chicago Press, 1941.

_____. "A Comment." *Economica*, n.s. 9 (November 1942):383-85.

_____. *The Road to Serfdom*. Chicago: University of Chicago Press, Phoenix Books, 1944.

_____. "Time Preference and Productivity: A Reconsideration." *Economica*, n.s. 12 (February 1945):22-25.

_____. *Individualism and Economic Order*. Chicago: University of Chicago Press, 1948.

_____. *The Counter–Revolution of Science*. New York: Free Press of Glencoe, 1955.

_____. *The Constitution of Liberty*. Chicago: University of Chicago Press, 1960.

_____. *The Sensory Order*. Chicago: University of Chicago Press, Phoenix Books, 1963.

_____. *Studies in Philosophy, Politics, and Economics*. New York: Simon & Schuster, Clarion Books, 1969.

_____. "Three Elucidations of the Ricardo Effect." *Journal of Political Economy* 77 (March/April 1969):274-85.

_____. *Law, Legislation and Liberty*, Vol. I: *Rules and Order*. Chicago: University of Chicago Press, 1973.

_____. ed. *Collectivist Economic Planning*. London: George Routledge & Sons, 1935.

Hicks, John R. "A Reconsideration of the Theory of Value." Part 1. *Economica*, n.s. 1 (February 1934):52-76.

_____. *Value and Capital*. 2d ed. Oxford: Oxford University Press, Clarendon Press, 1946.

_____. *Critical Essays in Monetary Theory*. Oxford: Oxford University Press, Clarendon Press, 1967.

_____. *Theory of Economic History*. New York: Oxford University Press, Galaxy Books, 1969.

_____. "A Neo–Austrian Growth Theory." *Economic Journal* 80 (June 1970):257-81.

_____. *Capital and Time: A Neo–Austrian Theory*. Oxford: Oxford University Press, Clarendon Press, 1973.

Hicks, J. R., and Weber, W., eds. *Carl Menger and the Austrian School of Economics*. Oxford: Oxford University Press, Clarendon Press, 1973.

Hirshleifer, J. *Investment, Interest, and Capital*. Englewood Cliffs, N.J.: Prentice–Hall, 1970.

————. "Where Are We Now in the Theory of Information?" *American Economic Review* 63 (May 1973):31-39.

————. "Exchange Theory: The Missing Chapter." *Western Economic Journal* 11 (June 1973):129-46.

Hurwicz, Leonid. "The Design of Mechanisms for Resource Allocation." *American Economic Review* 63 (May 1973):1-30.

Hutt, W. H. *Keynesianism: Retrospect and Prospect.* Chicago: Henry Regnery Co., 1963.

————. *A Rehabilitation of Say's Law.* Athens, Ohio: Ohio University Press, 1974.

Jaffé, William. "Walras' Theory of *Tâtonnement*: A Critique of Recent Interpretations." *Journal of Political Economy* 75 (February 1967):1-19.

Kaldor, Nicholas. "Capital Intensity and the Trade Cycle." *Economica*, n.s. 6 (February 1939):40-66.

————. "The Trade Cycle and Capital Intensity: A Reply." *Economica*, n.s. 7 (February 1940):16-22.

————. "Professor Hayek and the Concertina Effect." *Economica*, n.s. 9 (November 1942):359-85.

Kauder, Emil. *A History of Marginal Utility Theory.* Princeton: Princeton University Press, 1965.

Keynes, J. M. "A Rejoinder." *Economic Journal* 41 (September 1931):412-23.

————. "A Reply to Dr. Hayek." *Economica* 11 (November 1931):387-97.

————. *The General Theory of Employment, Interest, and Money.* 1936 Reprint. New York: Harcourt, Brace & World, Harbinger Books, 1965.

————. "Relative Movement of Real Wages and Output." *Economic Journal* 49 (March 1939):34-52.

Keynes, Milo, ed. *Essays on John Maynard Keynes.* New York: Cambridge University Press, 1975.

Kirzner, Israel M. *An Essay on Capital.* New York: Augustus M. Kelley, 1966.

————. *Competition and Entrepreneurship.* Chicago: University of Chicago Press, 1973.

Knight, Frank H. "Capital, Time, and the Interest Rate." *Economica*, n.s. 1 (August 1934):257-86.

_____. "Comment." *Journal of Political Economy* 43 (October 1935):625-27.

Kuhn, Thomas S. *The Structure of Scientific Revolution*. Chicago: University of Chicago Press, 1963.

Kuhn, W. E. *The Evolution of Economic Thought*. 2d ed. Cincinnati: South–Western Publishing Co., 1970.

Lachmann, Ludwig M. "A Reconsideration of the Austrian Theory of Industrial Fluctuations." *Economica*, n.s. 7 (May 1940):179-96.

_____. "The Role of Expectations in Economics as a Social Science." *Economica*, n.s. 10 (November 1943):12-23.

_____. *Capital and Its Structure*. London: G. Bell & Sons for the London School of Economics, 1956.

_____. *Macro–economic Thinking and the Market Economy*. Hobart Paper No. 56. London: Institute of Economic Affairs, 1973.

Lachmann, Ludwig M., and Snapper, F. "Commodity Stocks in the Trade Cycle." *Economica*, n.s. 5 (November 1938):453-54.

Lakatos, Imre, and Musgrave, Alan, eds. *Criticism and the Growth of Knowledge*. Cambridge: Cambridge University Press, 1970.

Lange, Oskar; McIntyre, Francis; and Yntema, Theodore; eds. *Studies in Mathematical Economics and Econometrics*. Chicago: University of Chicago Press, 1942.

Leijonhufvud, Axel. *On Keynesian Economics and the Economics of Keynes*. New York: Oxford University Press, 1968.

_____. "Effective Demand Failures." *Swedish Journal of Economics* 75 (1973): 27-48.

Lindahl, Eric, ed. *Selected Papers on Economic Theory*. London: George Allen & Unwin, 1958.

Lutz, Friedrich A., and Mints, Lloyd W., eds. *Readings in Monetary Theory*. Homewood, Ill.: Richard D. Irwin, 1951.

Machlup, Fritz. "Professor Knight and the 'Period of Production.'" *Journal of Political Economy* 43 (October 1935):577-624.

_____. "The Period of Production: A Further Word." *Journal of Political Economy* 43 (October 1935):808.

————. "Friedrich von Hayek's Contributions to Economics." *Swedish Journal of Economics* 76 (1974):498-531.

Makower, H., and Baumol, William J. "The Analogy Between Producer and Consumer Equilibrium Analysis." *Economica*, n.s. 17 (February 1950):63-80.

Marget, Arthur W. "Review of Friedrich A. Hayek, *Prices and Production*; and *Preise und Produktion*." *Journal of Political Economy* 40 (April 1932): 261-66.

McGee, John S. *In Defense of Industrial Concentration*. New York: Praeger Publishers, 1971.

Mill, John Stuart. *Principles of Political Economy*. Edited by Sir William Ashley. Clifton, N.J.: Augustus M. Kelley, 1973.

Mises, Ludwig von. *The Theory of Money and Credit*. N 2d ed. Translated by H. E. Batson. Irvington–on–Hudson, N.Y.: Foundation for Economic Education, 1971.

————. " 'Elastic Expectations' and the Austrian Theory of the Business Cycle." *Economica,* n.s. 10 (August 1943):251-53.

————. *Human Action*. New Haven: Yale University Press, 1949.

————. *Human Action*. 3d ed. Chicago: Henry Regnery Co., 1966.

Moggridge, D. E., ed. *The Collected Writings of John Maynard Keynes*. Vols. 5 and 6. London: St. Martin's Press, 1971.

Myrdal, Gunnar. *Monetary Equilibrium*. London: William Hodge & Co., 1939.

Nuti, Dominico Mario. "On the Rates of Return on Investment." *Kyklos* 27 (1974):345-69.

O'Driscoll, Gerald P., Jr. "The Specialization Gap and the Ricardo Effect: Comment on Ferguson." *History of Political Economy* 7 (Summer 1975):261-69.

————. "Hayek and Keynes: A Retrospective Assessment." Iowa State University Working Paper No. 20. Ames, Iowa: Photocopy, 1975.

————. "Spontaneous Order and the Coordination of Economic Activities." Menlo Park, Calif.: Photocopy, 1976.

Patinkin, Don. *Money, Interest and Prices*. 2d ed. New York: Harper & Row, 1965.

Pesek, Boris P., and Saving, Thomas R. *Money, Wealth and Economic Theory*. New York: Macmillan Co., 1967.

Phillips, A. W. "The Relation Between Unemployment and the Rate of Change of Money Wage Rates in the United Kingdom, 1861-1957." *Economica,* n.s. 25 (November 1958):283-99.

Phillips, C. A.; McManus, T. F.; and Nelson, R. W. *Banking and the Business Cycle.* New York: Macmillan Co., 1937.

Pirenne, Henri. *Economic and Social History of Medieval Europe.* New York: Harcourt, Brace & World, Harvest Books, 1970.

Ricardo, David. *Principles of Political Economy.* Edited by F. W. Kolthammer. New York: E. P. Dutton, 1948.

_____. *Works of David Ricardo.* Vol. 3. Edited by Piero Sraffa. Cambridge: Cambridge University Press, 1951.

Richardson, J. Henry. "Real Wage Movements." *Economic Journal* 49 (September 1939):425-41.

Robbins, Lionel. *The Great Depression.* London: Macmillan & Co., 1934.

_____. *An Essay on the Nature and Significance of Economic Science.* 2d ed. London: Macmillan & Co., 1935.

_____. *Autobiography of an Economist.* London: Macmillan & Co., 1971.

Robertson, D. H. "Mr. Keynes' Theory of Money." *Economic Journal* 41 (September 1931):395-411.

_____. *Essays in Monetary Theory.* London: P. S. King & Son, 1971.

Rothbard, Murray N. *Man, Economy and State.* 2 Vols. Princeton: D. Van Nostrand Co., 1962.

_____. *America's Great Depression.* Princeton: D. Van Nostrand Co., 1963.

Rotwein, Eugene, ed. *David Hume: Writings on Economics.* Madison: University of Wisconsin Press, 1970.

Schumpeter, Joseph A. *A History of Economic Analysis.* New York: Oxford University Press, 1954.

Seligman, Ben B. *Main Currents in Modern Economics.* 3d ed. New York: The Free Press of Glencoe, 1963.

Shackle, G. L. S. *The Years of High Theory.* Cambridge: Cambridge University Press, 1967.

Shenoy, Sudha R., ed. *A Tiger by the Tail.* London: The Institute of Economic Affairs, 1972.

Smith, Adam. *An Inquiry into the Nature and Causes of the Wealth of Nations*. Edited by Edwin Cannan. New York: Modern Library, 1937.

Sowell, Thomas. *Classical Economics Reconsidered*. Princeton: Princeton University Press, 1974.

Sraffa, Piero. "Dr. Hayek on Money and Capital." *Economic Journal* 42 (March 1932):42-53.

Stigler, George J. *Production and Distribution Theories*. New York: Macmillan Co., 1941.

———. *The Theory of Price*. 3d ed. New York: Macmillan Co., 1966.

———. *The Organization of Industry*. Homewood, Ill.: Richard D. Irwin, 1968.

Stigler, George J., and Boulding, Kenneth E., eds. *Readings in Price Theory*. Homewood, Ill.: Richard D. Irwin, 1952.

Streissler, Erich, et al., eds. *Roads to Freedom*. New York: Augustus M. Kelley, 1969.

Tarshis, Lorie. "Changes in Real and Money Wages." *Economic Journal* 49 (March 1939):150-54.

Thompson, Earl. "The Theory of Money and Income Consistent with Orthodox Value Theory." Los Angeles: Mimeographed, 1972.

Thompson, James H. "Mill's Fourth Fundamental Proposition: A Paradox Revisited." *History of Political Economy* 7 (Summer 1975):174-92.

Thorn, Richard S., ed. *Monetary Theory and Policy*. New York: Random House, 1966.

Thornton, Henry. *An Inquiry into the Nature and Effects of the Paper Credit of Great Britain*. Edited by F. A. Hayek. London: George Allen & Unwin, 1939.

Tobin, James. "Friedman's Theoretical Framework." *Journal of Political Economy* 80 (September/October 1972):852-63.

Tsiang, Sho-Chien. *The Variations of Real Wages and Profit Margins in Relation to the Trade Cycle*. London: Sir Isaac Pitman & Sons, 1947.

———. "Rehabilitation of Time Dimension of Investment in Macrodynamic Analysis." *Economica*, n.s. 16 (1949):204-17.

Walras, Léon. *Elements of Pure Economics*. Translated by William Jaffé. New York: Augustus M. Kelley, 1969.

Wicksell, Knut. *Lectures on Political Economy*. 2 Vols. Edited by Lionel Robbins. London: George Routledge & Sons, 1935.

_____. *Value, Capital, and Rent*. Translated by S. H. Frowein. London: George Allen & Unwin, 1954.

Wilson, Tom. "Capital Theory and the Trade Cycle." *Review of Economic Studies* 7 (June 1940):169-79.

Yeager, Leland. "The Keynesian Diversion." *Western Economic Journal* 11 (June 1973):150-63.

Yohe, William P., and Karnosky, Denis S. "Interest Rates and Price Level Changes, 1952-69." *Federal Reserve Bank of St. Louis Review* 51 (December 1969):18-38.

INDEX

The Studies in Economic Theory Series

Capital, Interest, and Rent: Essays in the Theory of Distribution by Frank A. Fetter, edited with an introduction by Murray N. Rothbard.
ISBN: 0684-3 (cloth); 0685-1 (paper)

The Economic Point of View by Israel M. Kirzner
ISBN: 0656-8 (cloth); 0657-6 (paper)

America's Great Depression by Murray Rothbard
ISBN: 0634-7 (cloth); 0647-9 (paper)

The Economics of Ludwig von Mises: Toward a Critical Reappraisal edited with an introduction by Laurence S. Moss.
ISBN: 0650-9 (cloth); 0651-7 (paper)

The Foundations of Modern Austrian Economics edited with an introduction by Edwin G. Dolan
ISBN: 0653-3 (cloth); 0647-9 (paper)

Capital, Expectations and the Market Process: Essays on the Theory of the Market Economy by Ludwig M. Lachmann, edited by Walter E. Grinder
ISBN: 0684-3 (cloth); 0685-1 (paper)

If you are unable to obtain these books from your local bookseller, they may be ordered direct from the publisher.

Sheed Andrews and McMeel, Inc.
6700 Squibb Road
Mission, Kansas 66202

Professor Gerald Patrick O'Driscoll, Jr, was born in 1947 and was graduated from Fordham University summa cum laude in 1969. He was awarded an M.A. in 1971 and a Ph.D. in economics in 1974 from the University of California at Los Angeles. His several areas of specialization include monetary theory, capital theory, law and economics, and the history of economic thought. His article "The American Express Case: Public Good or Monopoly?" appeared in the *Journal of Law and Economics* (1976). Recently his statement of "The Ricardian Nonequivalence Theorem" appeared in the *Journal of Political Economy* (1977), and his article on "The Specialization Gap and the Ricardo Effect: Comment on Ferguson" was published in *History of Political Economy* (1975). He is a frequent contributor to symposium volumes; an essay on stagflation coauthored with Sudha Shenoy was published in *Foundations of Modern Austrian Economics*, one of the volumes in "Studies in Economic Theory."

Currently O'Driscoll is editing a volume of essays on Adam Smith's *Wealth of Nations* to be published by the Iowa State University Press in 1978. At present he is serving as Assistant Professor of Economics at Iowa State University. He formerly taught at UCLA and at the University of California at Santa Barbara.